KD

Wharfedale
and
Nidderdale

THE SOUTHERN
YORKSHIRE DALES

Andrew Bibby

The Ramblers

FRANCES LINCOLN

The Freedom to Roam guides
are dedicated to the memory of
Benny Rothman

Frances Lincoln Ltd
4 Torriano Mews
Torriano Avenue
London NW5 2RZ
www.franceslincoln.com

Wharfedale and Nidderdale
Copyright © Andrew Bibby 2006

Photographs on frontispiece, pages 12–13, 72–3, 90–91, 110–111, 132–3 © Andrew Bibby; photographs on pages 18–19, 30–31, 44–5, 50–51, 58–9, 82–3, 98–9, 103, 126–7, 144–5 © John Morrison; photograph on pages 34–5 © Chris Ellison, Yorkshire Dales Green Lanes Alliance; photograph on pages 62–3 © Vincent Lowe; photograph on page 75 © Jeff Cowling, Craven Pothole Club; photograph on page 87 © Youth Hostels Association; photograph on pages 154–5 © David Raven; illustration on page 160 © Martin Bagness

Lyrics from 'The Manchester Rambler' song by Ewan MacColl used by kind permission of Peggy Seeger and of the publisher Harmony Music Ltd

Reproduced by permission of Ordnance Survey on behalf of HMSO. © Crown copyright 2005. All rights reserved. Ordnance Survey Licence number 100043293.

First published by Frances Lincoln 2006

British Library Cataloguing in Publication Data
A catalogue record for this book is available from the British Library

ISBN 0-7112-2553-2
Printed and bound in Singapore by Kyodo Printing Co.
9 8 7 6 5 4 3 2 1

Frontispiece photograph: Near Halton Gill, Littondale

Contents

Before you go – a checklist

- *Are access land restrictions in place?*
  Access land may be subject to temporary or permanent restrictions. Check at www.countrysideaccess.gov.uk or on 0845 100 3298.

- *Are weather conditions appropriate?*
  When poor weather is forecast, it may be sensible to postpone some of the walks in this book.

- *Do you have suitable equipment?*
  High ground can be significantly colder and more exposed than valley areas. A map and compass are recommended.

- *Does someone know where you are going?*
  If walking in a remote area, it is a good idea to leave details of your route and time of return.

- *Do you want to take a dog?*
  In general, you should assume that you will *not* be able to take dogs on open country. Most of the moors covered by this book have dog-exclusion orders in place. Check on the website or helpline given above.

- *Are birds nesting?*
  Between March and June open country is home to many ground-nesting birds. To find out where conservation restrictions are in force, check on the website or helpline given above.

Acknowledgements

The author gratefully acknowledges the assistance given him by a wide range of individuals and organizations, and is particularly grateful for the help offered by Kate Conto and Dan French of the Ramblers' Association and Kate Cave and Fiona Robertson at Frances Lincoln. Also much appreciated has been help given by staff of Yorkshire Dales National Park, staff of Nidderdale AONB, Peter Bancroft, Andrew Carter and staff of Yorkshire Water, Duncan Morrison (Above and Below), Rodney Waddilove, Jerry Pearlman, Angie Cairns, Mike Bartholomew (Yorkshire Dales Green Lanes Alliance), Mike Gill (Northern Mine Research Society), Anne Hoggarth, Paul Ticher, Jane Smith, Richard Blakeley, Nigel Smith, Colin Speakman, Ray Wilkes, John Robinson, Gwen Goddard, Joanna Bibby Scullion and Jane Scullion.

Series introduction

This book, and the companion books in the series, celebrate the arrival in England and Wales of the legal right to walk in open country. The title for the series is borrowed from a phrase much used during the long campaign for this right – Freedom to Roam. For years, it was the dream of many to be able to walk at will across mountain top, moorland and heath, free of the risk of being confronted by a 'Keep Out' sign or being turned back by a gamekeeper.

The sense of frustration that the hills were, in many cases, out of bounds to ordinary people was captured in the song 'The Manchester Rambler' written by one of the best-known figures in Britain's post-war folk revival, Ewan MacColl. The song, which was inspired by the 1932 'mass trespass' on Kinder Scout when walkers from Sheffield and Manchester took to the forbidden Peak District hills, tells the tale of an encounter between a walker, trespassing on open land, and an irate gamekeeper:

He called me a louse, and said 'Think of the grouse',
Well I thought but I still couldn't see
Why old Kinder Scout, and the moors round about,
Couldn't take both the poor grouse and me.

The desire, as Ewan MacColl expressed it, was a simple one:

So I'll walk where I will, over mountain and hill
And I'll lie where the bracken is deep,
I belong to the mountains, the clear running fountains
Where the grey rocks rise ragged and steep.

Some who loved the outdoors and campaigned around the time of the Kinder Scout trespass in the 1930s must have thought that the legal right to walk in open country would be won after the Second World War, at the time when the national parks were being created and the rights-of-way network drawn up. It was not to be. It was another half century before, finally, Parliament passed the Countryside and Rights of Way Act 2000, and the people of England and Wales gained the legal right to take to the hills and the moors. (Scotland has its own traditions and its own legislation.)

We have dedicated this series to the memory of Benny Rothman, one of the leaders of the 1932 Kinder Scout mass trespass who was imprisoned for his part in what was deemed a 'riotous assembly'. Later in his life, Benny Rothman was a familiar figure at rallies called by the Ramblers' Association as once again the issue of access rights came to the fore. But we should pay tribute to all who have campaigned for this goal. Securing greater access to the countryside was one of the principles on which the Ramblers' Association was founded in 1935, and for many ramblers the access legislation represents the achievement of literally a lifetime of campaigning.

So now, at last, we do have freedom to roam. For the first time in several centuries, the open mountains, moors and heaths of England and Wales are open for all. We have the protected right to get our boots wet in the peat bogs, to flounder in the tussocks, to blunder and scrabble through the bracken and heather, and to discover countryside which, legally, we had no way of knowing before.

The Freedom to Roam series of books has one aim: to encourage you to explore and grow to love these new areas of the countryside which are now open to us. The right to roam freely – that's surely something to celebrate.

Walking in open country – a guide to using this book

If the right and the freedom to roam openly are so important – perceptive readers may be asking – why produce a set of books to tell you where to go?

So a word of explanation about this series. The aim is certainly not to encourage walkers to follow each other, ant-like, over the hills, sticking rigidly to a pre-determined itinerary. We are not trying to be prescriptive, instructing you on your walk stile by stile or gate by gate. The books are not intended as instruction manuals but we hope that they will be valuable as *guides* – helping you discover areas of the countryside which you haven't legally walked on before, advising you on routes you might want to take and telling you about places of interest you will be passing along the way.

In areas where it can be tricky to find routes or track down landmarks, we offer more detailed instructions.

Elsewhere, we are deliberately less precise in our directions, allowing you to choose your own particular path or line to follow. For each walk, however, there is a recommended core route, and this forms the basis on which the distances given are calculated.

There is, then, an assumption that those who use this book will be comfortable with using a map – and that, in practice, means one of the Ordnance Survey's 1:25 000 Explorer series of maps. As well as referring to the maps in this book, it is worth taking the full OS map with you, to give you a wider picture of the countryside you will be exploring.

Safety in the hills

Those who are already experienced upland walkers will not be surprised if at this point we put in a note on basic safety in the hills. Walkers need to remember that walking in open country, particularly high country, is different from footpath walking across farmland or more gentle countryside. The main risk for walkers is of being inadequately prepared for changes in the weather. Even in high summer, hail and even snow are not impossible. Daniel Defoe found this out in August 1724 when he crossed the Pennines from Rochdale, leaving a calm clear day behind to find himself almost lost in a blizzard on the tops.

If rain comes the temperature will drop as well, so it is important to be properly equipped when taking to the hills and to guard against hypothermia. Fortunately, walkers today have access to a range of wind- and rain-proof clothing which was not available in the eighteenth century. Conversely, in hot weather you should take sufficient water to avoid the risk of dehydration and hyperthermia (dangerous overheating of the body).

Be prepared for visibility to drop when (to use the local term) the clag descends on the hills. It is always sensible to take a compass. If you are unfamiliar with basic compass-and-map work, ask in a local outdoor equipment shop whether they have simple guides available or pick the brains of a more experienced walker.

The other main hazard, even for walkers who know the hills well, is that of suffering an accident such as a broken limb. If you plan to walk alone, it is sensible to let someone know in advance where you will be walking and when you expect to be back – the moorland and mountain rescue services which operate in the area covered by this book are very experienced but they are not psychic. Groups of walkers should tackle only what the least experienced or least fit member of the party can comfortably achieve. Take particular care if you intend to take children with you to hill country. And take a mobile phone by all means, but don't assume you can rely on it in an emergency, since some parts of the moors and hills will not pick up a signal. (If you can make a call and are in a real emergency situation, ring 999 – it is the police who co-ordinate mountain and moorland rescues.)

If this all sounds off-putting, that is certainly not the intention. The guiding principle behind the access legislation is that walkers will exercise their new-won rights with responsibility. Taking appropriate safety precautions is simply one aspect of acting responsibly.

Access land – what you can and can't do

The countryside which is covered by access legislation includes mountain, moor, heath, downland and common land. After the passing of the Countryside and Rights of Way Act 2000, a lengthy mapping process was undertaken, culminating in the production of 'conclusive' maps which identify land which is open for access. These maps (although not intended as guides for walking) can be accessed via the Internet, at www.countrysideaccess.gov.uk. Ordnance Survey maps

Note: Each walk has been graded, on a scale of 🥾 to 🥾 🥾 🥾 🥾 🥾 , for the degree of difficulty involved. In general, walks are judged more difficult if they are (a) longer in mileage, and/or (b) involve more rough walking (across open moorland rather than on established footpaths), and/or (c) pose more navigational problems or venture into very unfrequented areas. But bear in mind that all the walks in this book require map-reading competence and some experience of hill walking.

published from 2004 onwards also show access land.

You can walk, run, birdwatch and climb on access land, although there is no new right to camp or to bathe in streams or lakes (or, of course, to drive vehicles). The regulations sensibly insist that dogs, where permitted, are on leads near livestock and during the bird-nesting season (1 March to 31 July). However, grouse moors have the right to ban dogs altogether and in much of the area covered by this book you can anticipate that this may be the case (for more information, watch for local signs).

Barden Moor (Walk 7) and Barden Fell (Walk 8) are the only two areas in the

Yorkshire Dales where voluntary access agreements were negotiated prior to the introduction of a general right to roam. The terms of the voluntary access agreements, which are slightly different from those covering land opened up under the 2000 Act, remain in force for the time being. Both moors have had a 'no dogs' rule in place for many years and this will continue to be applicable.

Access legislation also does not include the right to ride horses or bikes, though in some areas there may be pre-existing agreements that allow this. More information is available on the website given above and, at the time of writing, there is also an advice line on 0845 100 3298.

Barden Moor from Barden Fell

The access legislation allows for some open country to be permanently excluded from the right to roam. 'Excepted' land includes military land, quarries and areas close to buildings, and in addition landowners can apply for other open land to be excluded.

To the best of the authors' knowledge, all the walks in the Freedom to Roam series are either on legal rights of way or across access land included in the official 'conclusive' maps. However, you are asked to bear in mind that the books have been produced right at the start of the new access arrangements, before walkers have begun to walk the hills regularly and before any problems have been ironed out. As access becomes better established, it may be that minor changes to the routes suggested in these books will become appropriate or necessary. You are asked to remember that we are encouraging you to be flexible in the way you use the guides.

Walkers in open country also need to be aware that landowners have a further right to suspend or restrict access to their land for up to twenty-eight days a year. (In such cases of temporary closure there is normally still access on public holidays and on most weekends.) Notice of closure needs to be given in advance and the plan is that this information should be readily available to walkers, it is hoped at local information centres and libraries and also on the countryside access website and at popular entry points to access land. This sort of set-up has generally worked well in Scotland, where arrangements have been made to ensure that walkers in areas where deer hunting takes place can find out when and where hunting is happening.

Walkers will understand the sense in briefly closing small areas of open countryside when, for example, shooting is in progress (grouse shooting begins on 12 August) or when heather burning is taking place in spring. Once again, however, it is too early in the implementation of the access legislation to know how easily walkers in England and Wales will be able to find out about these temporary access closures. It is also too early to know whether landowners will attempt to abuse this power.

In some circumstances, additional restrictions on access can be introduced – for example, on the grounds of nature or heritage conservation, following the advice of English Nature or English Heritage.

Bear these points in mind, but enjoy your walking in the knowledge that any access restrictions should be the exception and not the norm. If you find access unexpectedly denied while you are walking in the areas suggested in this book, please accept the restrictions and follow the advice you are given. However, if you feel that access was wrongly denied, please report your experience to the countryside service of the local authority (or national park authority, in national park areas) and to the Ramblers' Association.

Finally, there may be occasions when you choose voluntarily not to exercise your freedom to roam. For example, many of the upland moors featured in these books are the homes of ground-nesting birds such as grouse, curlew, lapwing and pipit, who will be nesting in spring and early summer. During this time, many people will decide to leave the birds in peace and find other places to walk. Rest assured that you will know if you are approaching an important nesting area – birds are good at telling you that they would like you to go away.

Celebrating the open countryside

Despite these necessary caveats, the message from this series is, we hope, clear. Make the most of the new legal rights we have been given – and enjoy your walking.

Introduction

Do the Yorkshire Dales really need any introduction? Here, after all, is some of the best-loved and most-visited countryside in northern England. Visit, say, Bolton Abbey, Malham Tarn or a village such as Grassington or Kettlewell and, even out of season, you are very unlikely not to find yourself in the company of others who have also come to enjoy the particular pleasures of the Dales.

The Yorkshire Dales have had plenty of time to get used to visitors. The story of tourism here goes back at least two centuries, to the time when – at least for those with leisure – the idea of the countryside was undergoing a radical change. The Romantic movement marked the start of a new interpretation of what could be considered beautiful in nature. Indeed, in some respects Romanticism actually created the concept of natural beauty which still influences us so much today. You could argue that without the approach to the countryside which came in with Romanticism there would be no national parks today. No Pennine Way. And no Freedom to Roam guides either, come to that.

The Yorkshire Dales contained plenty to satisfy that early Romantic craving: ruins of old castles and abbeys, wild scenery, dashing waterfalls, sublime views. And so, two hundred or more years ago, a new class of visitor arrived in this part of northern England – the tourists who came to have their sensibilities engaged and their feelings aroused. Among them were some familiar names we now associate closely with the era of Romanticism: the poet William Wordsworth and the artist J.M.W. Turner, for example, both of whom will receive further mention later in this book (see pages 27, 97 and 101). There are many others who could be added to this list. One of the first artists of the period to come to the Dales was the fine watercolourist Thomas Girtin, who made a lengthy tour of the area in 1796, sketchbook in hand. Girtin was born, like Turner, in 1775 and was already well established as an artist when he died aged only twenty-seven. He is remembered best for Turner's often quoted tribute that, 'If Tom had lived, I should have starved.'

On Thomas Girtin's itinerary in 1795, as on Wordsworth's and Turner's when they came a few years later, were the ruins of the medieval priory Bolton Abbey in its spectacular setting beside the River Wharfe. At that date, Girtin probably had the place more or less to himself. But turn the clock forward to the end of the nineteenth century, when tourism had become a much more demotic pursuit, and the situation is rather different. By then, this stretch of Wharfedale had developed into one of the most popular places of escape for those who lived in Leeds, Bradford and the other crowded and polluted wool towns of West Yorkshire. As the nineteenth century ended and working conditions improved, ordinary people began to find that they had the free time – on Saturday afternoons, Sundays and mill holidays – to begin to explore the countryside. The development of new forms of transport such as the train and the bicycle meant that they also had the means to get there. Bolton Abbey station was opened in 1888 and rapidly found itself inundated by the thousands who would pour off the trains at holiday times. The story is that it was impossible for station staff to collect tickets individually; they simply gathered them up by the bucket-load.

The majority of visitors to the Dales may come today by car, but at the start of the twenty-first century Bolton Abbey remains as popular a destination as ever. In fact, it could be said to possess a kind of symbolic status, representative of the beauty of the Dales. Marie Hartley and Joan Ingilby, writing in 1956 in their book *The Yorkshire Dales*, put it like this: 'Bolton Abbey means to most people in the West Riding a pause in living, a sparkling, idyllic pause; it means summer afternoons by a rippling river, green pastures, and the priory ruins casting over their environment an extraordinary peace; it means a landscape of natural grace . . . .'

This Dales landscape is one we probably feel we know well, a special combination of broad green valleys, dotted with limestone walls and field barns, and a jumble of little villages.

The distinctive colour palette of the Dales is one of the things that gives the area its beauty: the particular green of the fields in the valleys, the particular grey of the stone. In a rapidly changing world it is a landscape which can seem, reassuringly, to have always been there, part of our country's heritage.

But at this point we need to be cautious. The Dales landscape we enjoy so much today is not a timeless one; indeed in many respects it is a relatively modern construct. The dry-stone walls which criss-cross the countryside are the result of the enclosure of the former common lands of each parish, a process which only came to an end at roughly the same time as Wordsworth, Turner, Girtin and their contemporaries were visiting the Dales. The period between 1760 and 1845 (and particularly the years either side of 1800) was the time when parliamentary enclosures redrew the field patterns of villages up and down the Dales. Grassington, for example, had its enclosure award in 1778, Linton in 1792–3, Malham in 1845.

This was a period of intense agricultural reform. In Burnsall and Threshfield, around 1700 acres of common and pasture

Watlowes dry valley, above Malham Cove

land were enclosed; in Conistone and Kettlewell, 8000 acres were enclosed; in Appletreewick, over 6000 acres were affected. Part of the task of implementing these enclosure awards was the construction of geometric rows of boundary walls around the newly created fields. Enclosure also tackled the high moorland and 'waste', including much of the country over which access rights now operate in the Dales.

Even before the enclosure awards of the period around 1800, the landscape of the Dales had been changed by human activity. For example, most of the medieval open fields (cultivated in strip holdings) in the valley bottoms had been enclosed by voluntary agreement many years earlier when land was swapped or sold to create consolidated holdings. The fields created in this way can often be identified because they tend to be smaller and less regular in shape than those created later by formal enclosure.

Trace the story back century by century and the look of the landscape gradually changes again. In post-Conquest medieval times, much of the land in the southern Dales was shared between the powerful Norman landowners and the great monastic establishments, including Fountains Abbey, Jervaulx Abbey and Bolton Abbey. Some of the roads we use today – and in particular some of the moorland footpaths followed by walks in this book – would have been used in medieval times to allow monastic travellers to reach their landholdings. Not all the land was farmed; Langstrothdale and upper Littondale were dedicated as forests (that is, hunting estates) and the upper Wharfedale village of Buckden had its origins in Norman times as a forest settlement (see page 65).

The pattern of land settlement in the centuries before the Conquest can be deduced from place names. Anglian and Danish settlers arrived from the east and south, gradually building up the network of villages and farmhouse settlements that, to a large extent, has remained in place today. Places ending in -ley (wood, woodland clearing) and -ton (farmstead) suggest an original Anglian settlement; local examples include Ilkley, Skipton, Grassington and Linton. Place names ending in -by (farmstead, settlement) and -thorp (hamlet or smaller settlement) imply Danish origins. Later Viking arrivals account for the -thwaite (clearing) suffix, as in Yockenthwaite and Bouthwaite.

Still further back, there are traces of the presence of Romans in the Dales. The Roman fort at Bainbridge in Wensleydale lies outside the area directly covered by this book, but the Roman road from Ilkley to Bainbridge can be traced on its journey up Wharfedale (and, for a short time, will be followed by anyone undertaking Walk 4). And earlier still, evidence of prehistoric human activity can be found in the landscape today: examples are the early settlement remains such as those on the hillside above the Wharfe between Kettlewell and Grassington, earthworks such as Tor Dike at the head of Coverdale, and the circular 'henges' of stones like the one in Langstrothdale near Yockenthwaite.

So the idea that the Dales landscape is a natural, unchanging one needs careful qualification. So, too, does the suggestion that, in contrast to the obviously industrialized urban area on its doorstep, the Yorkshire Dales are a region of unspoiled countryside untouched by industrialization.

It's ironic, perhaps, that at exactly the same time as Romanticism was first 'discovering' the Dales, mining activity in this area was at its peak. People in the Dales have been helping themselves (sometimes with considerable difficulty) to the wealth beneath the soil for at least two millennia. Lead, in particular, has played a central part in the Dales story from Roman times onwards. It would be hard to overemphasize the importance which lead mining once had in the local economy, particularly in the eighteenth and nineteenth centuries.

It's difficult to remain ignorant of this past if you visit, say, Grassington Moor or Greenhow Hill near Pateley Bridge, two areas where the above-ground landscape has been rudely rearranged as a result of mining activities. In other parts of the southern Dales, the legacy of lead mining may be more easily overlooked, at least by casual visitors. But, as this book will attempt to point out, even areas of the Dales countryside which seem as remote and unindustrialized as any may well have a history of mining. Buckden Pike (Walk 4), for example, is now a deservedly favourite destination for walkers enjoying the peace of the upper Wharfe valley. Yet, not so many generations ago, this hillside would have been a place of work, both underground in the mine shafts and on the surface where lead ore had to be separated from the less valuable 'gangue' minerals and then transported to the smelt mills.

It's a similar story when it comes to coal. While the most important coal field in the Dales, in Arkengarthdale near the Tan Hill pub, is to the north of the area covered by this book, coal was also extracted over many centuries in the southern Dales. There were significant coal mines, for example, on Barden Moor (Walk 7), near Dallowgill (Walk 11) and on the high ground of Fountains Fell (Walk 2), where the miners worked on wild, often bleak moorland.

Not many people would necessarily choose to spend their weekends or holidays rambling around the derelict industrial areas of cities. So does the industrial past of the Dales mean that the area is any the less attractive for walkers? Not at all, judging by the numbers of people who bring their walking boots this way. Rather, an appreciation of this part of the Dales' history surely adds to the interest and pleasure that can come from walking these hills and valleys. In one respect, however, walkers should be vigilant. Mining involved digging shafts in the ground, and not every one of these shafts was properly capped when mining came to an end. When access rights were first introduced in 2005, there were some in the Dales who painted grim scenarios of the risks which open shafts might pose to casual walkers. The fact that this may have been a ploy by some landowners to try to evade the new legal right to roam does not mean that there is not an issue here. The answer is simply to take care when walking off footpaths and tracks in open country, and to watch your feet particularly in places shown on maps as having being formerly mining areas.

The new right to roam has increased the amount of land which the public can enjoy within the Yorkshire Dales National Park by an astonishing amount, from 4 per cent to about 63 per cent. The aim of the walks in this book is to make the most of these new opportunities. If you think you already know the Dales well, undertaking some of the walks may come as a surprise. Tackle Walk 9, for example, and you'll find yourself on wild, wide-open moorland near Blake Hill which even on the busiest weekends and holidays is likely to be deserted. The new access arrangements also add some welcome bonuses to more familiar walking areas: near Malham (Walks 1 and 2) and Buckden Pike (Walk 4), for example.

The focus is not just on the national park itself. The Nidderdale Area of Outstanding Natural Beauty, which is geographically part of the Dales and which many people say should have been included in the national park in the first place, is also covered by this book. Nidderdale is indeed outstandingly beautiful, and access gives many new walking opportunities. For the first time, for example, the public can legally pay a visit to the curious moorland couple, Jenny Twigg and her daughter Tib (Walk 10), while for a glimpse of a real Yorkshire oddity don't miss the bizarre Druid's Temple to be found in a wood close to the moors near Masham (Walk 12).

Bolton Abbey certainly features in this book, and with good reason. But so does quite a lot more.

WALK 1

A MALHAM CIRCUIT

DIFFICULTY 🥾 🥾   **DISTANCE** 7½ miles (12 km)

| MALHAM VILLAGE | JANET'S FOSS | GORDALE SCAR | GREAT CLOSE HILL | MALHAM TARN | PENNINE WAY | MALHAM COVE | MALHAM VILLAGE |

MAP OS Explorer OL2, Yorkshire Dales (Southern and Western) or Harveys Dales South

STARTING POINT Malham village (GR 901628)

PUBLIC TRANSPORT In summer, Malham village is served at weekends by buses from Skipton. At the time of writing, one direct bus runs on summer Sundays and Bank Holidays from Leeds and Bradford, and another from Preston, Blackburn and Burnley. Check online or locally for details of current winter weekend buses.

PARKING In the national park car park in Malham

A circular walk to four of Malham's best-known sights: Janet's Foss, Gordale Scar, Malham Tarn and Malham Cove. Most of this route is straightforward, on well-walked footpaths and bridleways. The only possibly tricky moment – and the reason for the walk meriting its second 'boot' – is the scramble (of about 12 ft/3.6 m) which is necessary up the rocks beside the Gordale Scar waterfall. This may be challenging

or even impossible in icy conditions or after very heavy rain.

▶ Cross Malham Beck (the stream which runs through the heart of Malham village) to pick up the Pennine Way heading south. Shortly afterwards turn left, following the signs to Janet's Foss **❶**.

■ Janet's Foss is a delightful waterfall in an attractive area of woodland, which is now in the ownership of the National Trust.

'Foss' comes directly from the old Scandinavian for waterfall, and is still used today in that sense in Norwegian and Icelandic. The names of many other waterfalls in the Yorkshire Dales and north of England make use of the same word, though the variant spelling 'force' is more common.

Janet herself, according to local legend, was a fairy (perhaps even the Queen of the Fairies) who lived behind the waterfall. The fairy legend

was known at least two centuries ago, being mentioned by Thomas Hurtley who wrote an early version of a guidebook to the area in 1786.

Hurtley also discusses Janet's Cave (called by him Gennett's Cave). According to him, this cave, across the pool, had at one time been occupied (presumably after the fairies left) by smelters who were engaged in smelting copper extracted from a mine at Pikedaw Hill, to the west of Malham village. Hurtley mentions the 'evident ruins of a smelt mill' near by.

Arthur Raistrick considers this claim in his 1983 booklet *Mines and Miners on Malham Moor*, pointing out that at first sight Janet's Cave is an unlikely centre for copper smelting, not least because of the considerable distance from Pikedaw. He concludes that the site was perhaps used for roasting (an initial step in the treatment of copper ore, before smelting), by those associated with the early copper mining industry. He writes, 'They almost

▶ Map continues northwards on page 29

certainly chose the cave at
Gordale for the abundance
of timber and water, both
lacking on Malham Moor. It
seems likely that some of the
ruins which Hurtley knew
were in the wooded gorge
just below Janet's Cave,
where indeed there are still a

few fragments of masonry
but not enough to be
recognisable as a building.'

▶ Follow the path from Janet's
Foss, turn right when the road is
reached and take the second
footpath on the left, signed to
Gordale Scar.

■ Gordale Scar ❷ has long been one of the celebrated sights of the southern Dales, sought out by visitors for well over two hundred years. William Wordsworth was here in 1807, for example, with his sister Dorothy. Another poet, Thomas Gray (the author of *Elegy Written in a Country Churchyard*), was an earlier visitor. He took in Gordale Scar on his way back south from the Lake District, making a day trip from his inn in Settle: 'The gloomy uncomfortable day well suited the savage aspect of the place, and made it still more formidable: I stayed there, not without shuddering, a quarter of an hour, and thought my trouble richly paid; for the impression will last for life.'

It has been visual artists rather than writers who have left the most striking records of Gordale Scar, however. The English Romantic artist James Ward, a close contemporary of Turner, exhibited in 1815 an enormous canvas entitled *Gordale Scar* which he had probably painted in 1812–14.

The work (now owned by the Tate and regularly, although not permanently, on public display) is moody and atmospheric, with a stormy sky visible behind the two rock faces of the Scar which frame the painting. The twentieth-century artist John Piper (remembered for, among other things, the magnificent stained-glass baptistery window of Coventry Cathedral) painted a particularly striking semi-abstract landscape, also called *Gordale Scar*, in 1943.

▶ There is a right of way through Gordale Scar, but to follow it you will have to clamber up to the left of the lower waterfall, using the handholds and footholds in the rock. Once up, the path becomes much more straightforward.

■ Gordale Scar becomes, if anything, even more impressive at this point. The valley, at the bottom of cliffs 150 ft (45 m) high, is explained by geologists as an underground cave system that was carved out by water before the ground above collapsed to create the gorge.

▶ The path continues up the left flank of Gordale Scar for about 1 mile (1.6 km). Turn right when you reach the by-road and immediately leave it to continue north on the bridleway signed to Arncliffe, passing the start of the famous green lane Mastiles Lane (see page 32) at Street Gate ❸. Leave the bridleway at Great Close Plantation and scramble up the side of Great Close Hill ❹.

■ Great Close Hill offers a wonderful viewpoint to look down on Malham Tarn below. This natural lake is perhaps a surprising sight in an area of pervious limestone. In fact, the lake has formed in a hollow of boulder clay and there is a bed of impervious slate below. The water is retained by a natural 'dam', a moraine of rocks, stones and earth carried here by glacial activity.

Malham Tarn House, visible to the north-west, was originally a shooting lodge which was put up in the eighteenth century. In the nineteenth century it was the home of the millionaire Walter Morrison, who entertained many notable visitors there, including (as almost every guidebook, not excepting this one, feels obliged to mention) the writer Charles Kingsley. He may have drawn on his trip to Malham when he later came to write *The Water Babies*. The building is now a field studies centre.

▶ Drop down from Great Close Hill (avoiding the steep drop directly west of the summit), to pick up the Pennine Way at the side of the tarn. Turn left to start the return journey, which will follow the Pennine Way all the way back to Malham village.

■ Close to the Pennine Way, a short way south of the Tarn, you will find the interesting phenomenon of Water Sinks ❺, where Malham Water (the outflow from the Tarn) disappears underground into the limestone. It might seem obvious to assume that this water re-emerges to form the stream which can be found at the bottom of Malham Cove, 1 mile (1.6 km) or so to the

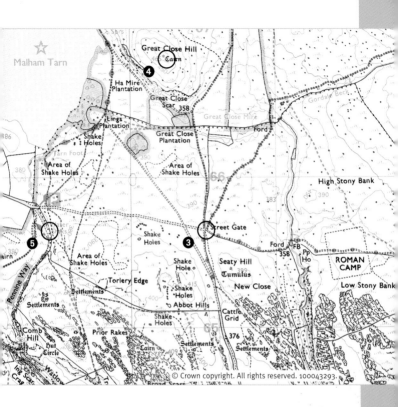

south. In fact, the labyrinthine series of passages and caves in the limestone carry the water considerably further, to the Aire Head spring south of Malham village (marked on OS maps).

▶ Continue on the Pennine Way through the Dry Valley of Watlowes, originally carved out by floodwater after the ending of the Ice Age, to reach Malham Cove ❻.

■ Malham Cove needs little introduction. This magnificent amphitheatre of limestone is 650 ft (200 m) wide and approaching 300 ft (85 m) high. Originally, before the water found its way underground through the limestone, water rushed down from Watlowes and tumbled over the side of the cove in what must have been an awe-inspiring sight (had anyone been around at that stage to be awe-inspired). What remains for us to look at today is impressive enough.

At the top of Malham Cove is a fine stretch of limestone pavement. The gaps between the limestone blocks (or 'clints') are known as 'grikes' or 'grykes' and provide important plant microhabitats. All the significant areas of limestone pavement in England, including at Malham, have now been protected by Limestone Pavement Orders (LPOs), which are issued by local planning authorities on the advice of government agencies. In some parts of the north of England, however, it is too late: recent decades have seen some priceless limestone habitats destroyed, mainly to fuel a

profitable trade in water-worn ornamental rocks in demand for garden rockeries.

Despite the use of LPOs, the illegal destruction of limestone pavements appears to be continuing. The Countryside and Rights of Way Act 2000 increased the maximum penalty for

destroying a protected pavement to £20,000, but it can be difficult to identify whether limestone rocks offered for sale have an illegal or legal provenance. One problem is that Ireland currently has much weaker protection in place and considerable quantities of limestone on sale in Britain have been imported, legally, from Ireland. It would, of course, be better if gardeners desisted from buying limestone rocks altogether.

▶ From Malham Cove, walk back down the valley and return to Malham village.

Janet's Foss, near Malham

Green lanes

Walking in the countryside is, most of the time, a quiet sort of activity, a chance to get away from the noise and pressure of urban living and enjoy a slower pace of life.

But not all the time. Sometimes walkers will find they are sharing their paths and tracks with others who have a rather different way of enjoying the countryside. There's been a boom in recent years in the popularity of 4x4 off-road vehicles and of trail bikes, and if you own one of these you naturally enough want to get it properly dirty with some real honest English country mud.

Many walkers in the Yorkshire Dales have learned to dread the growl in the distance which denotes that a group of bikers or off-road motorists is heading their way. Even on days when off-roaders are absent the results of their activity is all too often apparent in the deep ruts and churned mud which walkers have to pick their way around. The sport of 'mud plugging', as its adherents sometimes call it, could also be called 'mud making'.

Mastiles Lane, the old green lane linking Malham and Kilnsey, became a particularly notorious example of the problems caused by off-roading in the Dales. A beautiful track across Kilnsey Moor used once by medieval monks from Fountains Abbey, Mastiles Lane had degenerated to such an extent that many walkers voted with their feet and went elsewhere. But Mastiles Lane was not unique. The Dales has a host of other so-called 'green lanes' which off-roaders have discovered, including Top Mere Road near Kettlewell, Starbotton Cam Road which joins Top Mere Road on the moors above Wharfedale, and the byway from Coverdale into Nidderdale over Dead Man's Hill.

The reason why Mastiles Lane and these other tracks and byways have become such a mess in recent years is because, unfortunately, the law itself is a mess. The Act that created the national parks in 1949 arranged for every footpath (for use by walkers) and bridleway (for use by walkers, cyclists and horse riders) to be formally recorded on definitive maps. But the Act also came up with a curious type of route called a 'road used as a public path', or RUPP. What the Act didn't make clear was whether RUPPs – some of which had a proper sealed road surface, while others were effectively just rough country tracks – were available for use by motor vehicles.

More than thirty years on another Act, the Wildlife and Countryside Act 1981, tried to remove the ambiguity. Local authorities were required to examine each RUPP and to decide whether it carried vehicular rights. If so, the idea was to reclassify it as a 'byway open to all traffic', or BOAT. If not, RUPPs were supposed to be reclassified as bridleways or footpaths.

But the 1981 Act failed to achieve what was intended. In practice, the review turned out to be an enormous task and indeed in many areas local authorities have still not got to the bottom of the in-tray when it comes to considering the exact status of every one of their RUPPs. So, another two decades on, Parliament has tried again, using the Countryside and Rights of Way Act 2000 to invent the new legal concept of a 'restricted byway' – or, in other words, a byway which motor vehicles are not permitted to use.

The end result is that it's not easy to know, if you meet a trail biker or an off-roader when you're out walking, whether they have the right to be there or not. The confusion also means that the police are reluctant to bring prosecutions. Of course, the practical problems of policing a network of country lanes and tracks make matters even more difficult.

According to the national park authority itself, the use of green lanes by motorized vehicles is one of the most contentious issues which it has to deal with at present. The authority says that it would like to stop vehicle use on at least some of the green lanes within the national park, although the highway powers needed to do so are held by another body, North Yorkshire County Council. In spring 2003 a tentative first step was taken when the council banned vehicles from four local green lanes, including Mastiles Lane and Starbotton Cam Road/Top Mere Road. Initially the ban was only for a limited period, but the expectation is that these restrictions will be extended.

This is welcome news for the Yorkshire Dales Green Lanes Alliance, an organization set up in 2002 to bring together farmers, landowners, walkers and other country-lovers to oppose off-roading in the national park and Nidderdale. The Alliance reports that the banning order quickly had some effect in allowing the surfaces of the four selected green lanes to recover, although it adds that it will take centuries for the worst of the ruts to disappear. And, of course, a problem remains that not every biker or off-roader is obeying the 'No Entry' signs.

The real danger, according to the Green Lanes Alliance, is that the number of country byways legally used by motor vehicles will actually increase in the next few years. In theory, the opposite should be happening. In 2005, the government announced its plan to introduce yet more legislation; the fact that a track had historically been used by horse-drawn vehicles should not in itself mean that motor vehicles could also use it, the rural affairs minister said. The necessary legislation was making its way through Parliament as we went to press but the fate of claims already in the system for green lanes, bridleways and even footpaths to be reclassified as BOATs, byways open to all traffic, at present remains unclear.

It's been estimated that as many as 170 claims could be brought in the Dales for reclassification of green lanes and byways as BOATs. Although the new legislation may be enacted in time to protect some of these, the Green Lanes Alliance argues that the whole network of green lanes, including many which for years have been treated as bridleways and closed to vehicles, is extremely vulnerable to such claims.

In reply, off-roaders and trail bikers argue that they are simply

Trail bikers making mud in the Dales

using highways and byways which have been explored by generations of drivers and motorcyclists. As one 4x4 enthusiast put it, 'hordes of red-socked ramblers on their Sunday jaunts' have the run of all the footpaths and bridleways, and now the open countryside as well – so why should walkers begrudge motorists and bikers access to some green lanes and byways? The problem, he went on to argue, has been caused by 'a vocal and influential minority that wants motor vehicles out of "their" countryside'. Off-roaders, in other words, needed to get organized to fight back.

However, the difficulty faced by organizations such as the Trail Riders Fellowship, the Green Lane Association and the Land Access and Recreation Association, who claim to speak for responsible off-roaders, is that not everyone with an engine and a set of wheels in the countryside wants to be responsible. 'Cowboy' trail riders who leave the green lanes and tracks to head off cross-country in search of the muddiest and peatiest corners of the Dales are causing enormous environmental damage. Blubberhouses Moor, where large areas of moorland have been turned into what looks like a motocross circuit, is a particularly good – or bad – example. It may be exhilarating to rev the engine and see the wheels spinning, but at what long-term cost to the countryside?

In Kenneth Grahame's *The Wind in the Willows*, Mole and Ratty are not impressed by their first encounter with a motor car: 'Far behind them they heard a faint warning hum, like the drone of a distant bee. Glancing back, they saw a small cloud of dust, with a dark centre of energy, advancing on them at incredible speed, while out of the dust a faint "Poop-poop" wailed.' Mole and Ratty, one feels, would probably today be good candidates for joining the Yorkshire Dales Green Lanes Alliance. Toad, on the other hand, would clearly have other ideas: as he himself would put it as he set off for the byways and green lanes, Poop! Poop!

WALK 2

FOUNTAINS FELL

DIFFICULTY 👢 👢 👢   **DISTANCE** 10½ miles (17 km)

MALHAM TARN — PENNINE WAY — FOUNTAINS FELL — MALHAM TARN

MAP OS Explorer OL2, Yorkshire Dales (Southern and Western) or Harveys Dales South

STARTING POINT Quarry car park at Malham Tarn (GR 883672)

PUBLIC TRANSPORT In summer, Malham village is served at weekends by buses from Skipton. At the time of writing, one direct bus runs on summer Sundays and Bank Holidays from Leeds and Bradford, and another from Preston, Blackburn and Burnley. Also at the time of writing, a shuttle bus runs from Malham village (national park centre) to Malham Tarn on summer Sundays and Bank Holidays. Check online or locally for details of current winter weekend buses.

PARKING Informal parking for a limited number of cars in the old quarry

From Malham Tarn to Fountains Fell by the Pennine Way, with the option for some rough walking on the return leg. Fountains Fell can be exposed in poor weather.

▶ Turn right out of the quarry car park and immediately left, to find an old walled lane which runs alongside Tarn Moss. Turn right shortly afterwards, towards Tarn House.

■ Tarn Moss is a valuable wetland habitat which today is preserved as a nature reserve. This area of bog and fen developed around the point where streams bringing water off Fountains Fell disgorge their water into the tarn. However, Tarn Moss was significantly reduced in size after 1791 when the then owner of Malham dammed the tarn in order to increase the depth of the water by about 4 ft (1.2 m).

Now in the hands of the National Trust, Tarn Moss is carefully maintained as wetland through a management programme which includes scrub reduction and pool clearance.

Malham Tarn itself is a natural lake, which is a curious phenomenon in predominantly limestone country (see page 28).

▶ Walk along the drive that leads towards Malham Tarn House. Just past a number of estate cottages, turn left on to the Pennine Way ❶.

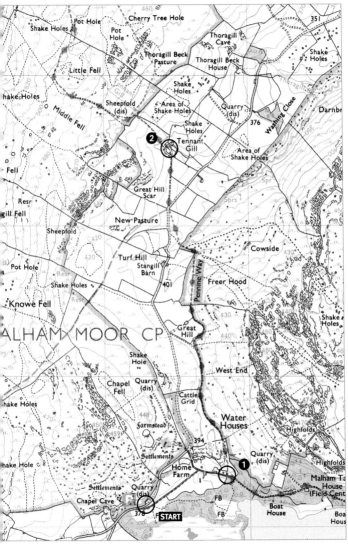

▶ Map continues northwards on pages 40–41

■ For the next 4 miles (6.4 km) or so the route follows Britain's most celebrated long-distance trail. The Pennine Way, officially opened in 1965, runs from Edale in the Peak District to Kirk Yetholm, just across the Scottish border, a distance of around 270 miles (435 km).

As Wainwright has put it, 'Officially Whitehall created the Pennine Way. But those who walk it should remember that it was one man who inspired, in his mind and by his patience and effort, the freedom they enjoy.' The man Wainwright refers to is Tom Stephenson, the writer and journalist (and later Secretary of the Ramblers' Association) who first floated the idea of what he called a 'long green trail' for walkers up the backbone of England in an article in the *Daily Herald* in 1935. As Wainwright records, 'Many were the difficulties and many were the objections but all were overcome in a long and tedious campaign, before Parliament set the seal

of authority on a recommendation by the National Parks Commission and gave approval to this first long-distance right of way for walkers.'

Incidentally, Wainwright walked this section of the Pennine Way in November 1966 and records that, somewhere on Fountains Fell,

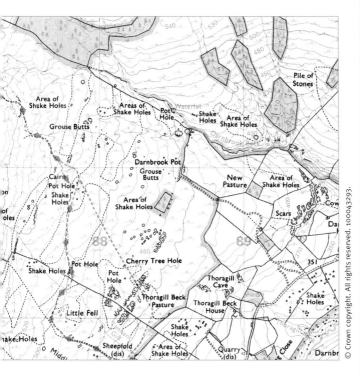

he lost a pipe. If you find an old tobacco pipe hiding in the vegetation, remember that it could have an illustrious past!

▶ Continue on the Pennine Way past Tennant Gill Farm ❷ and on to the slopes of Fountains Fell.

■ Fountains Fell gets its name not from any water features in the vicinity, but from its status in medieval times as part of the estate of Fountains Abbey. The abbey, which had been founded in the early twelfth century, acquired considerable landholdings in the Dales, reportedly owning ultimately over a million acres of land. Fountains Fell was used for sheep farming, and administered from the abbey's grange at Kilnsey. Mastiles Lane, the well-known green lane which runs from Kilnsey to Malham, was used by the abbey to access lands held around Malham.

For medieval landowners, the gift of a parcel of one's estate to a monastery was no doubt considered good insurance for the future protection of one's soul. As a consequence, Fountains Abbey was just one of a number of religious houses with major landholdings in the Dales area. Jervaulx Abbey had holdings in Wensleydale and other places. Bolton Priory had lands in upper Airedale (including other areas near Malham). Other abbeys, including those in Sawley, Byland and Bridlington, also held estates.

▶ The Pennine Way reaches the brow of Fountains Fell at a cairn ❸, before heading off north-westwards to Penyghent. At the summit cairn turn left. The next section of the route has been waymarked by the National Trust, using orange-banded posts.

■ Although Malham is today a centre for tourism, the region has an important industrial past. Lead was mined on the fells to the east of Malham Tarn, in the Kilnsey Moor and Hawkswick Clowder areas, while to the west of Malham village, near Pikedaw Hill, both copper and calamine were extracted (calamine, or smithsonite, is a zinc carbonate used in the manufacture of brass). On Fountains Fell, however, it was coal which was the target.

Fountains Fell is capped with millstone grit and within the layers of grit and shale are five seams of coal, four of them very thin. Coal had probably been taken from the hillside for use for many years, but the Fountains Fell Colliery, set up in 1807, was the first attempt to exploit the coal commercially. Once extracted, coal was taken down the hillside by packhorse and used for firing lime kilns and the nearby lead-smelting mill at Malham Moor. It was also converted to coke, with a coke oven built on the fell. This is still in very good condition and can be found to the right of the path.

The National Trust warns of uncapped mine shafts in this area. One impressive (fenced) shaft can be inspected at close quarters, just after turning off the Pennine Way.

▶ Follow the waymarks to another large cairn ❹.

■ This cairn is a good place, weather permitting, to enjoy the views. Penyghent is particularly close at hand, just across Silverdale.

▶ From the cairn continue following the orange-banded waymarks, turning left to make for another summit. Fountains Fell Tarn is away to the left. From here, continue downhill with the fell wall to your right.

Cross a wall coming up the hillside from the left, using the stones set in it. Beyond, head half-right to pick up the felltop

wall again. In due course, cross to the further side of the wall, where you will find a relatively well-walked path. Carry on for about 1 mile (1.6 km).

At the turning where the National Trust route heads left down the hill to return to Malham Tarn, it's worth continuing on the ridge for about another ⅓ mile (0.5 km), to reach a trig point ❺. There are more good views from here towards Penyghent.

From the trig point, cross back to the east side of the wall. The direction back to the starting point of the walk is now roughly south-eastwards. This is access land, so you can choose a route across open country. Alternatively, take the path which continues beside the wall south-westwards and then cut back north-eastwards on the bridleway shown on maps ❻. (To avoid any open country walking, a third alternative would be to return from the trig point to pick up the National Trust waymarked trail.)

■ The boggy millstone grit at the summit of Fountains Fell has now changed to limestone, as is clear both from the limestone outcrops and from the pots and shake holes (natural holes caused by weathering of limestone) which riddle the ground here. There are some particularly impressive pots to admire beside the fell wall just to the south of the trig point.

▶ The band of trees near Tarn Mere offers a target to aim for as you cross the last remaining area of open ground. A gateway gives access to the road just to the south-west of the quarry car park.

■ Just before reaching the

road, Chapel Cave (GR 881672) can be found. This sizeable opening in the hillside has been used by humans from Stone Age times.

The cave was excavated during 1996–9 as part of a project on prehistoric hunter-gatherers co-ordinated by the University of Bradford in conjunction with Michigan State University. Evidence was found that the cave had been used in mesolithic (middle Stone Age) times as a shelter for hunting parties.

Malham Tarn

WALK 3

HORSE HEAD PASS

DIFFICULTY 👟 👟 **DISTANCE 6 miles (9.6 km)**

HALTON GILL — HORSE HEAD GATE — ELLER CARR MOSS — COSH BECK — HALTON GILL

MAP OS Explorer OL30, Yorkshire Dales (Northern and Central) or Harveys Dales South

STARTING POINT Halton Gill, Littondale (GR 880765)

PUBLIC TRANSPORT No public transport to Halton Gill. Horse Head Pass can be approached from the Langstrothdale side by taking the bus to Buckden, although this adds almost 8 miles (13 km) of walking to the route.

PARKING Available for a limited number of cars opposite the village green

A short stretch of ridge walking between Littondale and Langstrothdale, offering views on both sides of the hill, before the more pastoral pleasures of Cosh Beck. A relatively straightforward route (the ridge section is exposed in poor weather).

▶ Walk out of Halton Gill towards Foxup, turning right almost immediately on to the grassy track which climbs up to Horse Head Pass.

■ The first part of the walk follows the historic route over Horse Head Pass linking Littondale and Langstrothdale. Indeed, a wooden sign marked 'Hawes' used to stand at the bottom of the track at Halton Gill.

The route over Horse Head Pass is one of the 'green lanes' in the Dales which have been used increasingly in recent years by 4x4 vehicles and trail bikes. The activity, though unpopular with most walkers and horse riders, was legal here until 2003 when a traffic regulation order banning vehicles was introduced by the county council (see page 34).

▶ Continue up the hillside to Horse Head Gate, at the top of the ridge ❶.

■ In their classic book *The Yorkshire Dales*, Marie Hartley and Joan Ingilby recount the tale of Halton Gill's parson, Thomas Lindley, who regularly rode or walked the Horse Head Pass on Sundays in order to take the service at the church in Hubberholme. He began his ministry at Halton Gill in 1807 and continued in the post for many years, making the round trip into Langstrothdale even when he was in his late seventies.

▶ Follow the wall boundary at the hill summit, making for the trig point. Shortly afterwards, cross through a gate to the further (Langstrothdale) side of the wall.

■ To the south the view is dominated by the long ridge of Fountains Fell (visited in Walk 2). Closer to hand, across the dale below, is Plover Hill, with the distinctive summit of Penyghent in sight just behind it for part of the walk. To the north-west (visibility permitting, of course!), Whernside, the highest of the Three Peaks, closes the view.

▶ Continue along the wall and cross back to the south side at the stile on the Halton Gill–Beckermonds footpath ❷. This path provides an alternative, quicker route back to the walk start. However, the suggested route carries on along the side of the wall for another ¾ mile (1.2 km) or so.

■ Robin Hood's Well, a spring in the hillside which feeds a mossy pool of water, lies just to the south of the wall on Eller Carr Moss. The name of the spring may be enough in itself to merit a short diversion to visit it.

This is by no means the only time Robin Hood makes an appearance on the maps of Yorkshire. A spring close to the River Wharfe between Grassington and Kilnsey bears the same name, as does yet another spring a little further to the north-east on Melmerby Moor near West Witton. There is also the celebrated Robin Hood's Well situated close to the top of Pendle Hill in Lancashire.

A companion volume in the Freedom to Roam series, *South Pennines and the Bronte Moors*, looks in more detail at the many allusions to Robin Hood which are found in place names in the north of England, and suggests that Nottinghamshire may not be the only county with a claim to the outlaw's memory.

However, in the case of springs like this one on Eller Carr Moss, thoughts of Robin Hood and his Merry Men may be misleading. One more plausible theory is that the Robin who is being

remembered is not the outlaw but the mischievous sprite Robin Goodfellow, who Shakespeare turned into the character Puck in *A Midsummer Night's Dream*. In times past, springs were often endowed with magical and spiritual properties. There is indeed something particularly magical about springs in limestone country such as this, where water appears from hillsides and

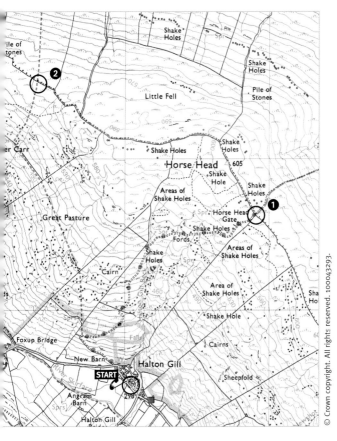

disappears back into the earth apparently randomly.

▶ Cross the fell wall ❸ and immediately follow it back down the hillside. Continue more or less due south, crossing the track to Cosh, to arrive at the waters of Cosh Beck ❹.

■ The historic farmstead at Cosh (which can be seen a little way to the right) at one stage belonged to Fountains Abbey, a fifteenth-century document referring to it as 'Grenefield Coche'.

Despite its isolation and the logistical problems of arranging for supplies to be delivered, particularly during the winter months, Cosh was continuously occupied for centuries. The tradition came to an end shortly after the Second World War and the fields belonging to Cosh are now worked by a neighbouring farm.

▶ Cross Cosh Beck and follow the right of way past a series of barns, before dropping down to cross the beck again near Foxup

Bridge. Continue back along the by-road to Halton Gill.

■ Ellergill Barn, at the foot of the Horse Head Pass track,

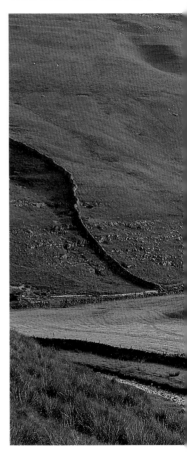

is one of two bunkhouses that can be found in Halton Gill. Previously semi-derelict, its conversion in 2002 preserved a number of original features and won a commendation in an architectural award scheme run by the Country Land and Business Association.

Between Malham Tarn and Arncliffe

WALK 4

BUCKDEN PIKE AND WALDEN HEAD

DIFFICULTY 👢 👢 👢 👢

DISTANCE 11½ miles (18.5 km)

| BUCKDEN | BUCKDEN PIKE | WALDEN HEAD | BROWN HAW | BUCKDEN PIKE | BUCKDEN |

MAP OS Explorer OL30, Yorkshire Dales (Northern and Central) or Harveys Dales South

STARTING POINT Buckden village (GR 942773)

PUBLIC TRANSPORT Buckden is served by regular buses from Skipton (Monday–Saturday) and by occasional buses on Sundays and Bank Holidays (including buses from Leeds).

PARKING In the national park car park in Buckden

The well-walked climb up the slope of Buckden Pike is followed by a venture into the peaceful and very little-known Walden valley. Some boggy moorland walking.

▶ From the national park car park in Buckden follow the bridleway north past Rakes Wood for about ⅔ mile (1 km).

■ The first few minutes of this walk almost certainly follow the line of a Roman road, probably constructed at the end of the first century AD during the period when Agricola was securing Roman rule in the north of England. The road's destination was the fort just outside Bainbridge in Wensleydale, known to the Romans as Virosidum. This fort, excavated several times by the University of Leeds, still has well-preserved foundations *in situ* below the ground.

The line of the Roman road, as far as it is known, follows that of today's bridleway past Rakes Wood, continuing round to the north-east to meet the modern B6160 at Cray High Bridge. From there it crosses the watershed over Stake Moss into Wensleydale, following the line taken today by Gilbert Lane. Beyond Stake Moss, the route passes Great Silky Top to join what is now High Lane above Stalling Busk.

In the other direction, south of Buckden, the line of the Roman road is probably close to, or in places identical to, that followed by the main road down the valley. The ultimate destination for the road was Ilkley, where it met up with a number of other Roman roads.

▶ Leaving the route of the Roman road behind, turn right ❶ at the signpost to Buckden Pike. Follow the track as it runs up the hillside, first in a north-easterly direction and then back south-eastwards, to arrive at the trig point at the top of the Pike ❷.

■ At 2303 ft (702 m) Buckden Pike is pipped in height by only about 6 ft (2 m) by its near neighbour Great Whernside.

Buckden Pike marks the watershed between the Wharfe river system and that of the Ure (the river which flows through Wensleydale). For the next part of this walk, therefore, the streams will be flowing northwards, together making up the waters of the Ure's tributary, Walden Beck.

▶ Cross the stile beside the trig point and continue down the hillside across rough open country for a few hundred yards (metres), heading due east. You will meet the bridleway between Starbotton and Walden after about five minutes' walking ❸. Turn left here and follow the bridleway down the hillside until you reach a shooting track.

The bridleway follows this track for a short way, before diverging again off to the right. Continue down the hillside, with views of the beautiful valley of Walden gradually opening up ahead. Pass a set of sheepfolds and carry on until you meet the road at Walden Head ❹.

■ Walden (just Walden, not Waldendale) is one of the quietest of the Yorkshire Dales and also one of the most lovely. Former editor of the *Dalesman* Bill Mitchell has gone on record to declare that it is his favourite dale of all, and his view might be shared more widely if more people took the trouble to discover Walden for themselves. It's certainly seen at its best when approached in this way, by foot from the south.

The one disadvantage that Walden has had for walkers in the past has been the relative lack of footpaths in the valley. The coming of access legislation has added enormously to the

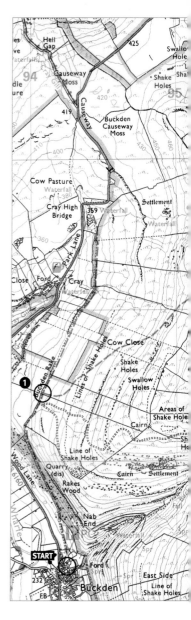

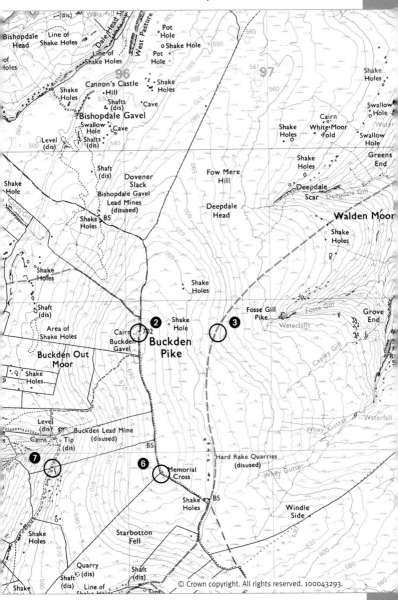

▶ Map continues eastwards on page 57

options, and the route back from Walden Head takes full advantage of this, returning on the ridge between Walden and Coverdale. Until 2005 this was the territory of gamekeepers, not available for the public to enjoy.

▶ Walk along the road past Grange Farm, and almost immediately turn right to take the shooting track which runs up the hillside. This track continues out of the first field but soon peters out. Head on, ever upwards. The best route is probably to follow the line of grouse butts. As you reach the high ground of Brown Haw ❺, turn right and follow the wire fence.

The moorland at Brown Haw is a sharp contrast to the pastoral beauty of Walden valley, and the views north towards Wensleydale disappear. But though the ground underfoot can be damp, navigation on the next part of the walk should not be a problem: simply keep beside the fence for the next 2½ miles (4 km) or so.

■ In due course, weather permitting, views will open up to the left, across the neighbouring valley of Coverdale to Little Whernside and Dead Man's Hill. It's also worth turning around periodically to admire the fine sweep of ridge over Brown Haw to Harland Hill in the distance.

▶ Once back on the saddle of Buckden Pike, turn right and make your way to the memorial cross ❻.

■ The sad story of the crash in January 1942 of an RAF Wellington bomber crewed by six Polish airmen has been recounted on the website www.buckdenpike.co.uk, run by Richard Fusniak. His father Joe (Jozef) Fusniak was the sole survivor of the accident.

The plane plunged into the side of Buckden Pike in very wintry weather conditions. On impact, the rear turret of the plane broke away from the fuselage, enabling Joe Fusniak to escape from the wreckage. However, he had broken his ankle in the crash and faced an agonizing walk

▶ page 60

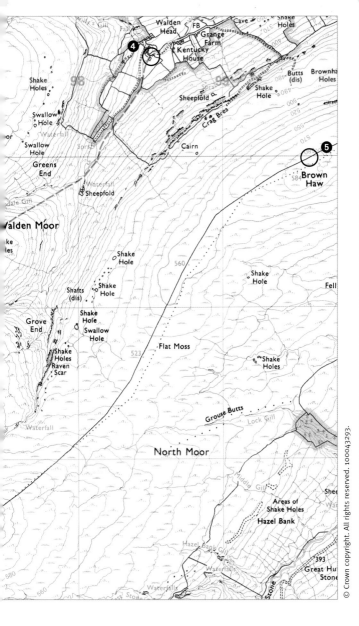

Upper Wharfedale, near Buckden

to find safety. The website records his experience:
'I could not see any further than six feet. The snowflakes were larger than my thumbnail, the size of a golf ball. I struggled for several hours, trying to make my way down treacherous slopes and over stone walls partially submerged in deep snow drifts. I remember a vertical cliff – nearly slid over the edge.'

Joe Fusniak believes he was saved when he saw a set of fox tracks heading down the hillside, in the opposite direction from that he had initially taken. He was eventually found on the road near the village of Cray. Unfortunately, by the time a search party reached the Wellington bomber, the last of his crew mates had died.

The cross was erected in 1973 and Joe himself played an active role in its construction. The fox head, made of bronze, at the foot of the cross commemorates the fox whose tracks helped Joe off the hillside.

▶ From the cross, make your way through the bogs and wet ground to the other side of the wall and head north along it to find the boundary stone (marked on OS maps) dated 1810. From here, drop steeply down the hillside, following the remains of the stone wall.

Divert over to the right if you want to look at the entrance to the level of the Buckden Gavel lead mine.

■ Levels, or adits, are the impressive tunnels burrowed into the hillside for sometimes considerable distances which can be found in many of the old mining areas of the Dales. The idea is a simple one: instead of sinking vertical shafts from the surface in order to reach the mineral veins, you start lower down the hillside and create what amount to horizontal shafts inwards.

Levels had a number of benefits: they could provide much-needed ventilation for existing underground workings, they could drain off water (flooding was a problem endemic to mine shafts) and they could also open up access to mineral veins which had previously been out of reach.

Lead mining had been undertaken north of Buckden Pike, in the Bishopdale Gavel area, from at least the late seventeenth century, but by the start of the nineteenth century the mines were nearing exhaustion. Work on the Buckden Gavel level began in 1803–4. Constructed 6 ft (1.8 m) high by 4 ft (1.2 m) wide it was typical of the levels of the time, which were large enough for horses to use. Iron rails were laid on the ground for horse-drawn wagons. Extending about 500 yards (500 m) into the hillside, the new level linked up with existing workings and also helped to give access to the lead ore in veins directly below Buckden Pike. The mine was worked until about 1883.

Much earlier, in 1698, a smelt mill had been constructed near the head of Buckden Beck, just below where the level would later be built. The smelt mill was excavated in 1974 by members of what is now known as the Northern Mine Research Society.

▶ Pick up the footpath **7** and follow it down the hill to return to Buckden village. Halfway down it is possible to cut straight down the open hillside, but be prepared for a steep final scramble.

The cloudberry

When the weather's poor and a cold wind is blowing in from the north, it's easy to feel that the Yorkshire Dales have migrated up to the Arctic regions. And that's perhaps why one of the most celebrated plants of the sub-Arctic is prepared to make its home in these hills.

The cloudberry (*Rubus chamaemorus*) is held in great affection by many Scandinavians. Indeed, when the Finns were choosing designs for their new Euro coins, it was this plant which they selected to illustrate the €2. It's partly that the little yellow or orange berries are such a striking sight in the wild. It's also perhaps that the berries can be good to eat: cloudberries are made into jam, ice cream and even, by the Finns, into a powerful alcoholic drink. Cloudberry coulis has been known to be served up in expensive restaurants with such northern delicacies as smoked elk's tongue, though if you are tempted to order this yourself aim to arrange for someone else to pay the bill.

Cloudberries are at the southernmost extent of their natural range in Britain. Although isolated plants have been discovered south of the Dales (in a nature reserve near Wrexham, for example), the children's story which has Wombles cloudberry harvesting on Wimbledon Common is unfortunately entire fiction. But cloudberries must have been present in the Dales for a very long time, since the plant has given its name to the hills of Great Knoutberry and Little Knoutberry, west of Hawes.

Cloudberries prefer high ground, and they are also particularly partial to a good bog. In fact, cloudberries are one of a number of species associated with blanket bogs, the peatland habitats created when plant material decomposes at a very slow rate in waterlogged ground. Peat bogs are likely to have begun developing in the Dales more than five thousand years ago, and in some places the accumulated peat can now be as deep as ten or even fifteen feet. It's possible that blanket bogs first began to form because early settlers on these hills cleared the original forest cover, although climate change may also have played an important part.

Nature conservationists are keen to protect these important peat habitats. They distinguish between healthy blanket bogs, where there is a good range of species, and those which are poor in species and in danger of drying out and becoming acidic

The cloudberry

grassland. (The latter type of bog can often be recognized by the presence of the wispy cotton-like seedheads of cottongrass.) A number of factors, including overgrazing and drainage work undertaken by landowners (particularly the cutting of moorland drainage channels or 'grips'), have contributed to the impoverishment of bogs. In some places old grips are now being deliberately blocked to encourage revegetation and reduce erosion.

A healthy blanket bog is one where peat is still slowly being formed, and it is here that the cloudberry is most likely to be found. It may well be sharing its habitat with other moorland plants, including the bilberry, cowberry, bearberry and cranberry. The best bogs of all are those with plenty of bog moss, and here you may also find the bog asphodel and the sundew, a carnivorous plant which traps insects with its sticky hairs.

The cloudberry is a creeping perennial related to the raspberry, the bramble and the wild strawberry. It is, as one guidebook puts it, a 'shy flowerer', but if you are lucky you may find a solitary flower on the plant in June and July. The flowers are white and are not dissimilar to the flowers of brambles and strawberry plants. The cloudberry is also pretty shy in terms of producing berries, which are about the same size as raspberries but harder to the touch.

It's best to forget any thoughts you might have of returning from a moorland walk with the materials for your own cloudberry ice cream, and to leave any berries you may be lucky enough to find for others to spot too. But it's not impossible that cloudberries may shortly become a more familiar part of our diet. Efforts have been made in Scandinavia to develop the commercial cultivation of the cloudberry, and very recently the Highland Council in Scotland has helped to set up a Northern Berries Group, the aim of which is to encourage crofters to consider growing the berries in the north of Scotland.

WALK 5

BIRKS FELL AND FIRTH FELL

DIFFICULTY 👢 👢 👢 **DISTANCE 10 miles (16 km)**

| BUCKDEN | BIRKS FELL | OLD COTE MOOR TOP | KETTLEWELL | STARBOTTON | BUCKDEN |

MAP OS Explorer OL30, Yorkshire Dales (Northern and Central) or Harveys Dales South

STARTING POINT Buckden village (GR 942773). The walk can also be tackled from Kettlewell (GR 969723).

PUBLIC TRANSPORT Buckden is served by regular buses from Skipton (Monday–Saturday) and by occasional buses on Sundays and Bank Holidays (including buses from Leeds).

PARKING In the national park car park in Buckden

A fine ridge walk on the high ground between Wharfedale and Littondale, followed by a riverside return along the Dales Way. Relatively straightforward, provided the weather is good.

■ Deer give Buckden both its name and its history. The village was originally established in Norman times by the Percy family who at that time held Langstrothdale Chase, the lands at the head of the Wharfe valley which were given over to hunting. Buckden was the administrative centre of the hunting estate.

▶ page 68

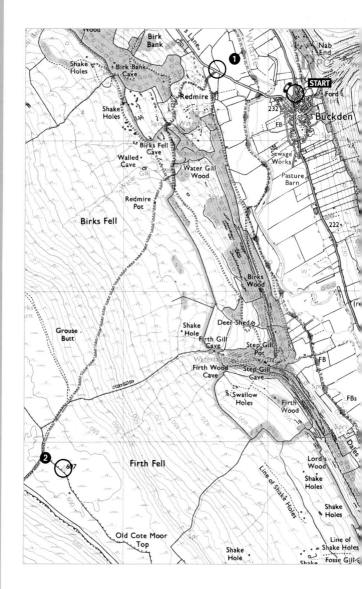

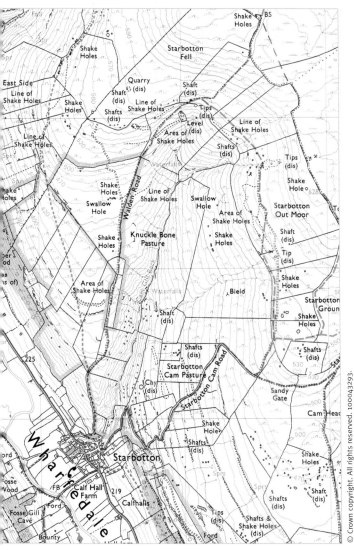

▶ Map continues southwards on pages 68–9

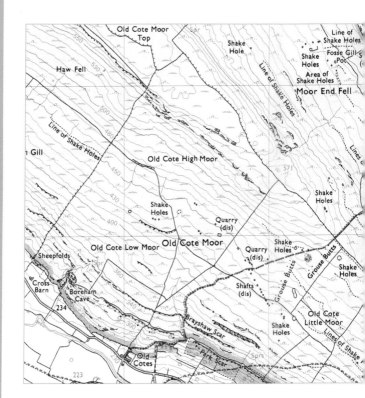

▶ From Buckden, follow the by-road towards Hubberholme and take the bridleway ❶ up the hillside past Redmire Farm.

■ The walk is initially on limestone country, and two separate caving systems have entrances very close to the bridleway just beyond Redmire. Birks Fell Cave is a long linear system which was first extensively explored by local cavers in the late 1960s. The underground stream passage extends for over 2 miles (3 km) in total and drops about 500 ft (150 m) in height.

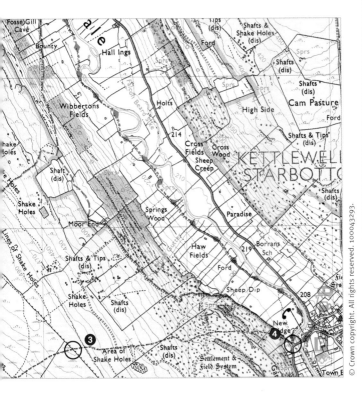

Redmire Pot, although close to Birks Fell Cave, provides an entrance to a separate, parallel cave system which emerges to the south-east in Birks Wood. It was explored in the late 1970s by members of Cambridge University Caving Club, who gained access using diving equipment. They commented on the fine collection of helictites (horizontally growing stalactites) which they found in the passages. This particular cave system extends for 1 mile (1.6 km), with a total depth of 385 ft (117 m).

▶ Continue up the bridleway, across the open moorland of Birks Fell and up the hillside. The ground becomes boggier, a clear indicator that the rock below has changed from limestone to millstone grit. Those who enjoy walking across open ground can divert off the track westwards to make for the waters of Birks Tarn. Otherwise keep on the bridleway until you meet and cross a fell wall. Shortly afterwards you will reach the brow of the hill. Turn left off the bridleway here to find the OS trig point ❷.

■ The trig point is at a height of 607 m (put another way, this means that, at 1991 ft, it just fails to break the 2000-ft mark). The climb from Buckden has involved more than 1250 ft (380 m) of ascent.

▶ Fortunately, from now on it's downhill almost all the way. A path of sorts runs off south-eastwards from the trig point across the open boggy ground of Old Cote Moor Top. In about ⅔ mile (1 km), you will reach another fell wall. Cross the wall

using the protruding stones and continue south-east along the ridge, keeping on the Wharfedale side of the wall.

■ From the ridge, there are fine views down to Littondale and to the fells beyond, with Penyghent a landmark about 6 miles (9.6 km) away to the west. In the other direction, across the Wharfe, rises Buckden Pike.

▶ The wallside track continues for another 2 miles (3 km) or so, crossed at one point by the Starbotton–Arncliffe path. In due course, Kettlewell comes into sight in the valley below.

Although the ridge can be followed for a further 1 mile (1.6 km) or so, the suggested route is to turn left at the point where the footpath from Arncliffe to Kettlewell crosses the fell wall at a stile ❸. Follow the path down the hill.

■ Once more, limestone is the dominant rock and the ground on the Wharfedale side of the ridge is riddled with shake holes created by rainwater working its way through the limestone.

As well as these natural holes, the hillside above Kettlewell and Arncliffe also has holes of a different kind, created by human effort. As in other parts of the Dales, these are the remains of the lead mining that took place from the late seventeenth century to the late nineteenth century. The most significant operation in this area was the Wharfedale Mine, which was formed by a number of Yorkshire businessmen in 1857 and ran until 1879.

▶ The path emerges on to the main road just across the Wharfe from Kettlewell. For the return route, take the footpath on the left which you reach immediately *before* the bridge ❹.

■ For the remaining 4 miles (6.4 km) or so, the route back to the starting point follows paths and tracks alongside the Wharfe. It forms part of the Dales Way, the waymarked long-distance trail from Ilkley to Bowness on Windermere.

The Dales Way is an excellent example of how initiatives taken by walkers at local level can grow into a successful national venture. It was in 1968 that the Dales-based writer Colin Speakman and his colleague in the West Riding Ramblers' Association Tom Willcock came up with the idea of a long-distance path which would link the Yorkshire Dales with the Lake District. Unlike the Pennine Way, which tends to search out the high ground wherever possible, the Dales Way is a relatively low-level route and this has made it popular with walkers who prefer pastoral landscapes. As Colin Speakman has written, 'The Dales Way isn't a route to be rushed. It isn't a challenge walk, it isn't a marathon and there are no prizes for anyone daft enough to do it within a certain time. This is a walk to take at a civilized, perhaps even gentle, pace.'

The Dales Way follows the Wharfe upstream from Ilkley before crossing over into Dentdale and then leaving the national park to head off into Cumbria. In all, the route is about 84 miles (135 km), with extensions at the south end to connect Ilkley with both Bradford and Leeds.

Colin Speakman's pioneering guide to the Dales Way, first published in 1970, remains in print today, one of several guidebooks dedicated to the route.

▶ Continue past the small village of Starbotton back to Buckden.

■ The River Wharfe is a delight to follow on peaceful summer days, but it is not always benign. One of the worst recorded floods was in June 1686, when both Starbotton and Kettlewell were badly damaged in the aftermath of a ferocious thunderstorm.

Birks Fell in winter

Going underground

Limestone does strange things to water. Rivers can disappear abruptly in limestone country, as at Water Sinks south of Malham Tarn (Walk 1) and at the River Nidd near Manchester Hole (Walk 10). Smaller streams, too, plunge suddenly and unexpectedly down shake holes, their water resurfacing sometimes miles further on.

In return, water does strange things to the limestone. The slightly acidic rainwater worms its way through cracks in the rock, widening them, tunnelling them out, carving subterranean watercourses, leaving these behind for new, deeper courses, creating stalactites and stalagmites, making caves. The process is measurable only in geological time, not human time. But the result today is that the Yorkshire Dales area boasts not only some of the finest limestone country in Britain but, underneath, some of the finest cave systems as well.

Humans lived in some of these caves in earliest times. Victoria Cave near Settle is known to have been occupied in the prehistoric era. Chapel Cave (Walk 2) near Malham Tarn is another site where traces of early human occupancy have been discovered.

But these days the caves of the Dales fulfil another role. The age of modern caving can perhaps be said to have begun in Britain in 1842 when John Birkbeck from Settle was lowered on a rope into the great hole of Gaping Gill near Ingleborough. He reached a ledge 190 ft (58 m) down, and made it back to the surface just before the strands of his rope severed. The feat was repeated a generation later, in 1882, by another courageous man, Alfred Clibborn, while the first descent of Gaping Gill's full 360 ft (110 m) was undertaken in 1895 by the famous French caver Edouard Alfred Martel.

At the bottom of Gaping Gill is the massive void known as Main Chamber, and the start of a network of many miles of passage. These include a connection to the neighbouring Ingleborough Cave system, first successfully negotiated in 1983.

Gaping Gill, and other legendary caving destinations including nearby Alum Pot (also first explored by John Birkbeck) and the extensive Lancaster-Easegill cave systems, are outside the

Robinson's Pot near Darnbrook, north of Malham

geographical area covered by this book and are dealt with in the sister Freedom to Roam guide *The Three Peaks and the Howgill Fells*. But the areas of Wharfedale and Nidderdale both also have extensive cave systems, some suitable for exploring by experienced potholers, some to be enjoyed by beginners.

Several of the walks in this book go close to the entrance points of these cave systems. Walk 10 in Nidderdale passes the large hillside openings of Manchester Hole and Goyden Pot, which give access to a complex labyrinth of chambers, river passages and rope pitches. In Wharfedale, the initial climb from Buckden village in Walk 5 passes close to the entrances to two separate systems, those of Birks Fell Cave and Redmire Pot.

A very expansive network of cave systems on the eastern side of the Wharfe valley carries water to a single resurgent spring, Black Keld south of Kettlewell. Among the caves linked to Black Keld are Rigg Pot (whose entrance is passed on the descent from Great Whernside in Walk 6), Langcliffe Pot and the extensive Mossdale Caverns, which in 1967 were the scene of the worst tragedy in British caving when six cavers died after the system unexpectedly flooded.

But it is perhaps on the ascent of Great Whernside from Kettlewell, close to the hostel of Hag Dike (Walk 6), that walkers may want to pause a moment and think of what lies below their feet. At some point here, more than 400 ft (120 m) below, runs the famous – or infamous – Dowbergill Passage.

Dowbergill Passage links Dow Cave (GR 985743) with Providence Pot (GR 993729) almost exactly a mile away across the moors. Dow Cave itself is classified as 'easy', a walk-in cave system which extends for about 1100 ft (335 m) and can be tackled by (escorted) beginners, provided they have a light and are prepared to wade in the stream and duck down in those places where the cave roof drops to about 4 ft (1.2 m) in height. Dow Cave is a beautiful limestone cave system with sets of stalagmites, stalactites and helictites, the curious fingers of calcium carbonate which emerge horizontally from the cave walls, often twisting and gyrating into strange shapes.

Dowbergill Passage is a different matter. Those who have undertaken the journey (and your author at this point admits to being reliant on the accounts of others) describe it as a classic caving trip – though some have also suggested that the last word should have a letter changed, to read 'trap'.

On charts of the caving system, Dowbergill Passage appears as a simple straight line, with Dow Cave at one end and Providence Pot at the other. Unlike other challenging caves, the passage does not require ladders, diving gear or any other specialist equipment. But the reality belies the idea of a straightforward through trip.

Terry Trueman and Ian Watson, two cavers who have written a detailed account of the crossing, talk of 'a never-ending nightmare of squeezes, frictionless, bottomless rifts, crumbling shale ledges, boulder chokes, mud and cold, cold deep water'. They go on: 'To this mixture can be added the cocktail of despair – total isolation, extreme frustration and utter exhaustion. Dowbergill Passage can be a very lonely and unforgiving place.'

Unfortunately, if not surprisingly, Dowbergill Passage is well known to the local cave rescue service who have had to deal with a number of call-outs over the years. In some instances, cavers have simply become too exhausted to continue. There is, however, also a risk of rock fall. Indeed, an unexpected boulder fall has led to at least one fatality in Dowbergill Passage.

Even if this all sounds off-putting, experienced cavers relish the challenge offered by the system. Dowbergill Passage was first explored end to end in 1955 by members of the local Craven Pothole Club, and since then many have made the journey. Generally, a successful through trip is likely to last several hours (much longer, of course, if you get lost or stuck). Having said that, very fit cavers have managed to complete the Dowbergill Passage in no more than two hours.

WALK 6

GREAT WHERNSIDE FROM KETTLEWELL

DIFFICULTY 👢 👢 👢 **DISTANCE 6 miles (9.6 km)**

KETTLEWELL → HAG DIKE → GREAT WHERNSIDE → SWEET HILL → LANGCLIFFE → KETTLEWELL

MAP OS Explorer OL30, Yorkshire Dales (Northern and Central) or Harveys Dales South

STARTING POINT Kettlewell village (GR 969723)

PUBLIC TRANSPORT Kettlewell is served by regular buses from Skipton (Monday–Saturday) and by occasional buses on Sundays and Bank Holidays (including buses from Leeds).

PARKING In the national park car park in Kettlewell

A brisk climb of 1475 ft (450 m) from the Wharfe valley to the summit of Great Whernside, followed by a more gentle descent through limestone outcrops.

▶ Take the lane which passes Kettlewell church and the Kings Head pub, continuing with the stream to your left. As you pass the last of the houses in Kettlewell, the tarmac gives way to a track. Shortly afterwards cross the stream and then turn right, following the sign for Providence Pot.

For the next 1 mile (1.6 km) or so the path follows the side of Dowber Gill Beck, past a series of small falls. This delightful stretch of upland walking leads to the entrance to Providence Pot ❶.

■ For experienced cavers, Providence Pot is a celebrated, indeed notorious, place to spend a few hours underground. Providence Pot is linked to Dow Cave (1 mile/1.6 km or so away to the north-west) by the Dowbergill Passage (see page 76).

For non-cavers, however, Providence Pot is simply the somewhat ugly concrete end of the entrance shaft, topped with a metal manhole cover.

▶ Turn left as Hag Dike Gill Beck comes in to join Dower Gill Beck, and then immediately clamber up out of the river valley. You will be able to find faint paths, heading across open ground in the direction of Hag Dike ❷.

Hag Dike, or Hag Dyke (both spellings are used), is a former farmhouse which has been turned into a scout hostel. It was almost derelict when it was given to the scouts of Ben Rhydding near Ilkley in 1947, and much loving care has been expended on the building to bring it back to life.

■ The Dowbergill Passage reputedly runs directly under Hag Dike's kitchen, about 420 ft (125 m) below.

▶ Just as you reach Hag Dike, turn right and find the track up the hill.

■ Although the route from Kettlewell to Great Whernside has been walked for very many years, until recently there was no legal right of way shown on the official footpath map of the area. This meant that as walkers climbed up the final flank of Great Whernside they ran the risk of being turned back.

Rodney Waddilove, an active member of the Ramblers' Association in the region, decided that it was time to get this unsatisfactory situation sorted out. Having failed to persuade the landowners informally to agree to a footpath, he and the Harrogate group of the Ramblers' put in a formal application to the national park authority for the definitive map to be amended. With the application went 167 submissions from individual walkers, collected with considerable effort from all over Yorkshire and indeed Britain, backing the application and confirming that the walkers had themselves used the route.

The bid to amend the map was heard by the national park in 1992. Initially Rodney Waddilove and his fellow walkers lost the motion, on the casting vote of a local farmer. It took an appeal to the Secretary of State and much more correspondence and effort before, finally,

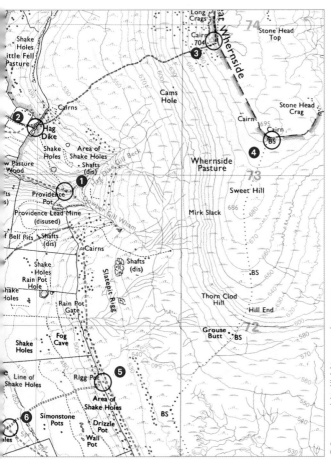

in 1997 word came back from London that the ramblers were right – there was indeed an historic right of way up to Great Whernside.

At the same time, Rodney Waddilove got in touch with Yorkshire Water, the landowner on the Nidderdale side of Great Whernside. Yorkshire Water helpfully agreed to dedicate a new right of way around the ridge to Little Whernside and Dead Man's Hill (see Walk 9), which would meet up with the newly agreed footpath from the Kettlewell side. The Ordnance Survey maps, which had previously shown the Great Whernside plateau bare of rights of way, were revised. Walkers were welcome on Great Whernside – and that was official.

Like all such battles it can be easy, once victory is achieved, to forget the work which went into it. Although the new access rights give the public the opportunity to roam at will on open country, formal rights of way in general offer greater legal protection.

It is a valuable achievement by Rodney Waddilove and his colleagues to have successfully registered these footpaths across the Great Whernside mountain plateau.

▶ A series of posts and cairns mark the way on to the summit ❸.

■ Great Whernside, at 2308 ft (704 m), is the highest of Wharfedale's hills, higher than nearby Little Whernside but (confusingly for some first-time visitors to the Dales) lower than Whernside, a few miles away to the west. The name refers to the fact

The familiar Wharfedale landmark of Kilnsey Crag

that the hills are formed of millstone grit, suitable for making millstone querns.

Great Whernside was the site of two aircraft crashes during the Second World War, one in November 1943 and another in May 1945. Small amounts of wreckage remain from these crashes, as well as detritus from a third crash in 1948.

▶ From Great Whernside, turn right to follow the path which runs southwards along the ridge. At a cairn ❹, the path tucks in to the right of a new wire fence, running almost due south down to Sweet Hill. Continue beside the fence as you gradually lose height.

Leave the fence eventually and cut across open ground for a short distance to find the fell wall. Make for the gate in the wall ❺ and then continue across the field, initially on a faint path and then on a much better defined farm track.

■ The millstone grit of the summit of Great Whernside has now changed back to limestone. The hillside here is a maze of shake holes and pots, including one just to the right of the track.

The water which disappears into the hillside here re-emerges close to the Wharfe river about 1 mile (1.6 km) south of Kettlewell, at the resurgence known as Black Keld (GR 974710) which is marked on OS maps as a spring.

▶ Some may want to take the footpath which the track meets ❻ back to Kettlewell. The suggested route, however, is to continue down the hillside, to explore the limestone outcrops overlooking Wharfedale. Various paths follow the edge of the rock outcrops northwards.

In due course, make for the gap in the field wall and follow the footpath back to the village of Kettlewell.

Porridge and postage stamps

Kettlewell, like so many other communities in both rural and urban Britain, had lost its post office. The old branch, which had been run from a kitchen in a private house in the village, closed in 2002, and that, most Kettlewell residents thought, was the last time that they'd ever have a post office on their doorstep. In future, it seemed, anyone wanting to post a parcel or buy foreign currency would have to make the journey down the dale to Grassington.

But over at the youth hostel, manager Judith Mallams had a different idea. There was a reception area in the hostel which she used when booking in overnight visitors. The building was regularly staffed during the day. So why not make use of her facilities? Why not move the post office to the youth hostel?

It was an inspired idea, though Judith knew it was not something the Youth Hostels Association had ever tried before. Fortunately, what she was proposing tied in very closely with the way that the YHA itself had been thinking. To be able to maintain its network of hostels in some of the country's most beautiful areas, the YHA knew that it needed to run its affairs profitably, and that meant diversifying and looking for new sources of income where appropriate. Managers were being positively encouraged to think creatively about how they could develop their hostels.

There is a difference between having a good idea, however, and being able to make it happen. Judith Mallams and her colleagues did their research and quickly realized that they needed a significant amount of money to be able to proceed. It wasn't just a case of making space among the piles of hostelling leaflets for a set of parcel scales: the builders would have to be called in. The old reception hatch, for example, would have to be properly fitted out with a glass screen, and important requirements of the Disability Discrimination Act would have to be met, including a new ramp to enable wheelchair users to access the counter.

It took two years to raise the £40,000 necessary to go ahead, with the funds finally coming from a range of separate sources, including local authorities, the Countryside Agency, the Post Office and the YHA. But with the finances finally in place the work commenced. The new Kettlewell post office, just inside the door of the youth hostel, opened for the first time in the summer of 2004.

Some days it's relatively quiet, with only a handful of customers. Other times, as Judith puts it, things can get manic. She recalls her first Christmas, when the parcels piled up behind the counter and for a short while, she says, her youth hostel resembled Santa's grotto. With opening hours from 10.30 am to 1.30 pm on Tuesdays to Saturdays, the post office fits in well with the more traditional work of making the hostel's overnight users feel at home.

There are advantages all round to the new arrangement. Although the hostel has been a feature of life in Kettlewell for years, the post office counter brings in many local people who had never previously passed through the front door. As well as helping to tie the hostel closer to the community, it also brings in welcome spin-off business: for example, one post office customer realized that the hostel could provide accommodation for guests who were coming to the village to attend her grand-daughter's wedding.

Kettlewell's post office arrangement also helps make the point that youth hostels are changing ('the idea that it's bare floorboards and twenty to a dormitory is years out of date,' Judith says). Like other hostels, Kettlewell no longer requires its visitors to be YHA members, and certainly not everyone staying meets the typical hosteller stereotype. In fact, the Kettlewell hostel tends to be popular particularly with families with young children, who can take advantage of the small family bedrooms. (The fact that the building is licensed also seems to go down well with parents.)

The 2001 foot and mouth outbreak caused enormous problems for the youth hostel movement, and subsequently a number of hostels in the Yorkshire Dales had to close their doors. Although the income from the post office is not enormous, it will provide a buffer against any future shocks like this and should help ensure that Kettlewell youth hostel will be able to remain open for many more years to come.

Kettlewell's youth hostel – and post office

WALK 7

BARDEN MOOR

DIFFICULTY 👢 👢 👢   **DISTANCE 10½ miles (17 km)**

BURNSALL
VILLAGE

NUMBERSTONES
END

CRACOE
OBELISK

RYLSTONE
CROSS

UPPER
BARDEN
RESERVOIR

BURNSALL
VILLAGE

MAP OS Explorer OL2, Yorkshire Dales (Southern and Western) or Harveys Dales South

STARTING POINT Burnsall village (GR 032612)

PUBLIC TRANSPORT Burnsall is served by buses from Ilkley and Grassington.

PARKING In the car park in Burnsall

A tough clamber up from Burnsall, but thereafter primarily well-walked paths and tracks across heather-clad Barden Moor. Choose a day with good visibility to enjoy the fine views. As with other access land, Barden Moor may be closed temporarily, particularly when shooting is taking place. Dogs are not permitted on the moor.

▶ Leave Burnsall village by the road towards Bolton Abbey, turning almost immediately right along a lane. Shortly afterwards, the lane becomes a track. Just before it peters out, turn left through a farm gate on to access land and head up the hillside, keeping a wall to your right. At the top, leave the field by another gate and find the faint path which snakes up (first half-right, then half-left) to the cairn at the top of the hill ❶.

■ Burnsall village's big day is the annual Burnsall Sports, held each year on an August Saturday. Outsiders who want to know exactly when to turn up should remember that it's quite straightforward: the first Saturday after the first Sunday after 12 August.

The celebration is held to commemorate the Feast of St Wilfrid, the seventh-century Northumbrian churchman to whom Burnsall church is dedicated, and locals claim there have been festivities in the village at this time of year since at least the Elizabethan era. These days, the activities are focused on the village green beside the River Wharfe. The daytime events normally consist of stalls and sideshows, a display by the local morris team, a fly-casting competition, children's races, Punch and Judy and an egg-throwing contest (keep well back). The most famous event, however, is the Burnsall Classic fell race which rounds off the day at 5 pm and which attracts some of the best fell-running athletes in the country.

Runners leave the village to race straight up the hillside (a little to the left of the route followed by this walk) to the cairn at the top. Thereafter comes the heart-stopping descent straight back down to Burnsall, including the moment when the fell wall has to be crossed (the fastest runners leap it).

The fell race claims to be the oldest in the country, and it certainly has been run for well over a hundred years. The story is that it was concocted by a group of villagers in the Red Lion pub one evening in 1870 (or 1847 or 1865 – dates vary). It seems that the route was first tried out by local runner Tom Young, who won a bet by running up to the cairn and back naked.

The most famous fell race took place in 1910 when the legendary fell runner Ernest

▶ page 92

Burnsall from Burnsall Fell

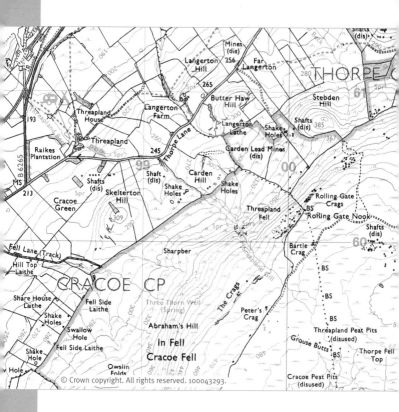

Dalzell completed the route in an astonishing 12 minutes and 59.8 seconds. His descent in particular, when he appeared to fly down the fellside, was considered superhuman, taking only 2 minutes and 42 seconds. For many years his time was questioned locally by those who felt that the stopwatch must have been misread.

Dalzell's record lasted for over half a century but has since been beaten by other runners. The current record, set in 1983 by John Wild, is 12 minutes 48 seconds.

It is also traditional that the day of Burnsall Sports is

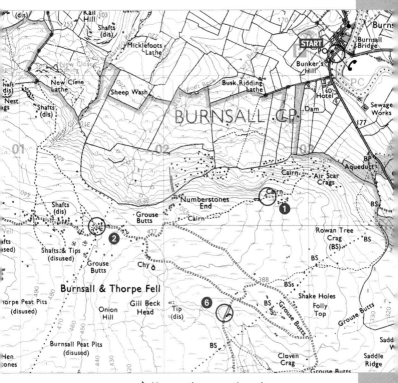

▶ Map continues southwards on pages 94–5

marked by the flying of a flag from the cairn. Since the 1930s the task of putting up the flag has fallen to the Fitton family, who gather with friends by the village green at around 7 am to make their way up the fell. As Chris Fitton has recounted, exactly what is flown can vary: 'The flag is, and always was, the great problem. No one can ever find it. Over the years it has taken the shape of an old cream bed sheet, a St George's flag and for many years a National Benzole flag. God only knows where that came from.' Once at the cairn, the top is dismantled, the flagpole inserted, the flag attached, the cairn rebuilt and the successful mission celebrated with a slug of whisky.

Though fell runners have no time to enjoy it, the view from the cairn is magnificent, with Burnsall in the foreground and upper Wharfedale stretching away to the north behind.

▶ From the cairn, continue westwards along the edge of the hillside to reach the rocky outcrop at Numberstones End. From here, a substantial stone-built estate building should be in sight over to the left. Make for this building, either directly across the moor or by continuing along the faint path close to the fellside wall for

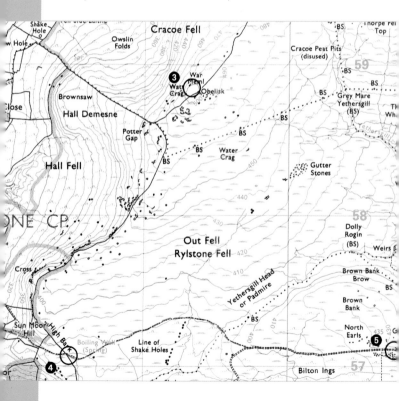

about ½ mile (0.8 km), cutting back left once you reach a well-walked path.

■ The estate building marks the site of what was once an extensive area of coal mining in this part of Barden Moor. The nearby stone shelter ❷ is a convenient place for walkers to pause and eat their sandwiches.

Barden Moor is part of the Duke of Devonshire's landholdings in the area. Like Barden Fell (visited in Walk 8), Barden Moor was subject to access agreements negotiated with the estate in 1968, so this beautiful stretch

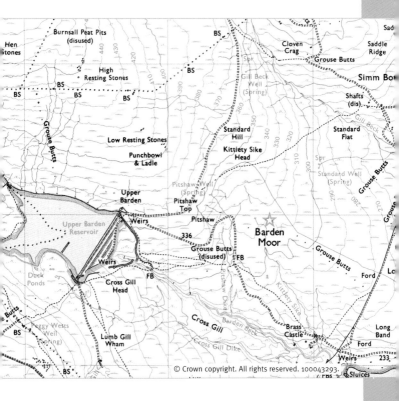

of moorland has become in recent decades a popular destination for walkers. The most well-walked areas, however, are those reached from Rylstone, Embsay or Barden Bridge, rather than from Burnsall.

The fine heather moorland, while it may look like a natural landscape, is in fact the result of careful and continual management by the estate to maximize opportunities for grouse shooting. One feature of moor management is regular heather burning that removes the older growth every few years. This is undertaken because grouse have a preference for the shoots of young heather.

Grouse suffer from intestinal problems and trays of grouse grit, designed to aid the birds' digestive systems, are a frequent sight on grouse moors. The grit may be medicated specifically to tackle intestinal worms. Well-managed grouse moors also try to maintain the bird population by reducing the number of predators. It is legal to snare or trap predators such as stoats, weasels, crows and rats.

▶ From the shelter follow the main track westwards. For the next 1 mile (1.6 km) or so there are magnificent views northwards to enjoy. The track eventually turns south-westwards and the views switch accordingly. Follow the track as it picks up a fellside wall, to reach the Cracoe obelisk ❸.

■ It's worth crossing the ladder stile to reach the obelisk, which enjoys a prominent position overlooking the valley below and the villages of Cracoe and Rylstone. It commemorates the thirteen local men who died in the First World War and the three who died in the Second World War.

▶ Continue south from the obelisk along the edge of the fell wall, passing an old boundary stone. This, carved with the letters C and R, marks the boundary between the Cracoe and Rylstone parishes. Carry on until you reach Rylstone Cross.

■ Rylstone Cross is modern, dating back only to 1995. It replaces a nineteenth-century cross which had fallen down early in the 1990s, to the concern of some people in the valley below who claimed it had mysteriously 'disappeared'. Visitors to the cross may want to ponder the appropriateness or otherwise of the plaque below which names the corporate sponsors involved in its funding.

The cross offers another good place to enjoy the views, this time to the west and south. Pendle Hill is a prominent landmark, about 16 miles (26 km) away to the south-west.

▶ Continue beyond the cross, turning left ❹ shortly afterwards on to the bridleway from Rylstone. Follow the bridleway for a good 1½ miles (2.5 km).

■ The bridleway across Barden Moor is linked to a tale from the sixteenth century, which Wordsworth turned into a poem after he had paid a visit to the area. The Norton family were local landowners, and the ruins of Norton's Tower, built by Richard Norton, can be found halfway up the hillside just to the west of the moor. Richard Norton unwisely participated in the Pilgrimage of Grace, the 1536 uprising against Henry VIII which opposed the break with the Church of Rome and the Dissolution of the Monasteries. The uprising was unsuccessful and one of Richard's sons, Francis, was later killed in retaliation.

Wordsworth's poem tells how Francis' sister Emily crossed the moor from Rylstone to visit her brother's grave at Bolton Priory in the company of a beautiful white deer, which the title of *The White Doe of Rylstone* commemorates. The legend had it that the deer continued to make the journey even after Emily's own death and was to be found every week in the churchyard at Bolton when services were taking place.

▶ page 100

Wordsworth later reported how the act of writing *The White Doe of Rylstone* had exacerbated a blister he had previously acquired from walking in tight shoes. 'I found the irritation of the wounded part was kept up by the act of composition . . . poetic excitement, when accompanied by protracted labour in composition, has throughout my life brought on more or less bodily derangement,' he wrote. Sadly, the pain may not have been entirely worthwhile, since most modern readers find the poetic epic of *The White Doe of Rylstone* almost unreadable.

▶ As Upper Barden reservoir comes into sight to the left, turn off the bridleway ❺ and take the track down to the reservoir dam. The Cracoe obelisk is a landmark above the moors to the west.

■ Upper Barden reservoir was opened in 1883, the culmination of engineering works which also included the construction, nine years earlier, of Lower Barden reservoir, a little further down Barden Beck.

Across Wharfedale are the moors of Barden Fell. Simon's Seat is a prominent landmark on the hillside opposite.

▶ Pass the Yorkshire Water building beside the dam at Upper Barden and immediately turn left off the approach road, taking a grassy track. Follow this for over 1 mile (about 2 km) to reach a small tarn ❻. The estate building visited earlier in the walk is now in sight again, high on the hillside beyond the tarn. The remains of a chimney can also be seen a little further down the hillside.

Beyond the tarn, cross a track. At a second track, turn right and immediately left, to pick up a small path which runs through the heather. This path, initially faint, later becomes waymarked with cairns. Continue until you meet a fellside wall and follow this down, passing into woodland to meet the road from Bolton Abbey about ½ mile (0.8 km) or so south of Burnsall.

The Strid

The priory ruins at Bolton Abbey and the beautiful riverside Strid Wood just to the north have attracted visitors of all kinds for at least two centuries. It was in 1810 that the Reverend William Carr, who was Rector of Bolton Abbey for fifty-four years, talked the sixth Duke of Devonshire into opening up this part of his estate to public visitors, and from then on the crowds never stopped coming. Turner and Landseer were among those who passed this way early in the nineteenth century, both transforming their visits into paintings. Turner's *Bolton Abbey from the South* can today be seen at the University of Liverpool Art Gallery.

Wordsworth also came here, in the summer of 1807, and two poems were the result. One is the lengthy *The White Doe of Rylstone* which, as argued on the previous page, is hardly Wordsworth at his most inspired. In a shorter poem, *The Force of Prayer; or, the Founding of Bolton Priory*, he retold the legend that the priory had been established by Cecily Romilly as an expression of her grief following the death of her son. He had died trying to jump across the Wharfe at the Strid, the point where the river dramatically narrows between rocks.

In the poem, Wordsworth imagines the son out hunting with his greyhound:

The pair have reached that fearful chasm,
How tempting to bestride!
For lordly Wharf is there pent in
With rocks on either side . . .

And hither is young Romilly come,
And what may now forbid
That he, perhaps for the hundredth time,
Shall bound across the Strid?

He sprang in glee, – for what cared he
That the river was strong, and the rocks were steep? –
But the greyhound in the leash hung back,
And checked him in his leap.

Young Romilly fails to make the jump:

The Boy is in the arms of Wharf,
And strangled by a merciless force;
For never more was young Romilly seen
Till he rose a lifeless corse.

Now there is stillness in the vale
And long, unspeaking, sorrow . . .

From Lady Romilly's grief comes a determination:

Long, long in darkness did she sit,
And her first words were, 'Let there be
In Bolton, on the field of Wharf,
A stately Priory!'

The stately Priory was reared;
And Wharf, as he moved along,
To matins joined a mournful voice,
Nor failed at evensong.

It's possible to question how well the poetic muse was operating when Wordsworth came to write about the Strid, but at least his verse can serve as a cautionary tale. Visitors today who might be tempted to emulate young Romilly should follow the advice given by the warning signs at the Strid and treat this place with respect.

Bolton Abbey

WALK 8

SIMON'S SEAT

DIFFICULTY 👢 👢   **DISTANCE 9¾ miles (15.7 km)**

| BOLTON ABBEY (CAVENDISH PAVILION) | STRID WOOD | CONY WARREN | SIMON'S SEAT | LORD'S SEAT | HAZLEWOOD MOOR | SOUTH NAB | BOLTON ABBEY (CAVENDISH PAVILION) |

MAP OS Explorer 297, Lower Wharfedale and Washburn Valley, or Harveys Dales East. Almost all the route is also covered by OS Explorer OL2, Yorkshire Dales (Southern and Western).

STARTING POINT Main visitors' car park beside the Wharfe, near the Cavendish Pavilion (GR 077552)

PUBLIC TRANSPORT Bolton Abbey village is served by buses from Ilkley and Grassington. There is a walk of 1 mile (1.6 km) to the walk start.

PARKING In the car park

An escape from the crowds at one of the busiest parts of the Dales on to the open fells.

▶ From the Cavendish Pavilion car park walk upstream alongside the Wharfe into Strid Wood. After a short distance, the river narrows dramatically at the Strid.

■ This area of Wharfedale forms part of the Bolton Abbey estate. The lands originally belonged to an Augustinian monastic order based at Bolton Priory, whose striking ruins occupy an impressive position beside the river just south of here. The priory was established in the mid-twelfth century and for four centuries dominated life in the southern Dales, where it was a major landowner. The nave of the priory church was saved from demolition during the Dissolution of the Monasteries in the reign of Henry VIII, and has now become incorporated in the local parish church.

Today the Bolton Abbey estate is part of the extensive landholdings controlled by the Cavendish family (the family name of the Duke of Devonshire), who also own Chatsworth House in Derbyshire and Lismore Castle in County Waterford in Ireland.

Strid Wood is an attractive area of woodland which has been popular with visitors for many generations (see page 101) and has now been declared a Site of Special Scientific Interest.

▶ Continue along the riverside beyond the Strid itself. Just before you reach Barden Bridge, cross the river by the castellated bridge known as the aqueduct ❶.

■ This bridge was constructed to hide a pipe which brings water across the Wharfe from the reservoirs in Nidderdale.

Upstream are the ruins of Barden Tower, built on the site of a hunting lodge in the late fifteenth century by Henry Lord Clifford. The tower was rebuilt in 1657 by the redoubtable Lady Anne Clifford (Lady Anne Clifford's status as a Dales legend is explored in the Freedom to Roam guide *Wensleydale and Swaledale*). The Clifford lands later passed by marriage into the possession of the Cavendish family.

▶ Walk up the hillside from the aqueduct, cross the minor road and enter open moorland at Cony Warren ❷. Keep to the track as it bends round to the right, to follow the edge of Lower Fell Plantation.

At this point, it's possible to scramble up to Carncliff Top. The easier walking, however, is to continue on the moor-edge path, enjoying the views which periodically open up towards upper Wharfedale.

After 1 mile (1.6 km) or so, the path is joined from the left ❸ by a forest track. Beyond here, a well-walked path heads off north-eastwards towards Truckle Crags.

■ Just to the west of Truckle Crags, in the heart of the heather, is the intriguingly named Devil's Apronful, a prehistoric site marked on maps as a cairn. The site is in the shape of a rough circle about 20 yards (20 m) across.

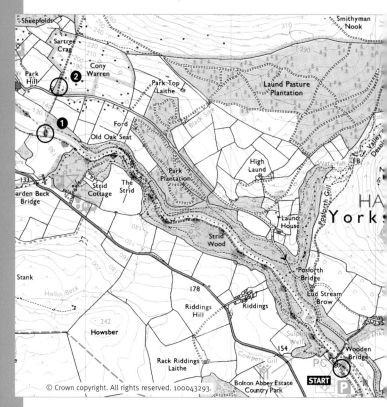

▶ Make your way on to the rocky outcrop known as Simon's Seat ❹ and enjoy the dramatic views down to the valley directly below and to upper Wharfedale away to the north-west.

■ Simon's Seat is a prominent landmark in the southern Dales, and a popular target for walkers, fell runners and climbers. Quite who Simon was is not clear. Some suggest a druidical association, while the Victorian writer Halliwell Sutcliffe spins a yarn about the shepherd called Simon

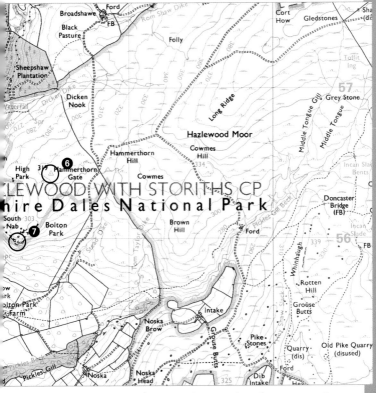

▶ Map continues northwards on pages 108–9

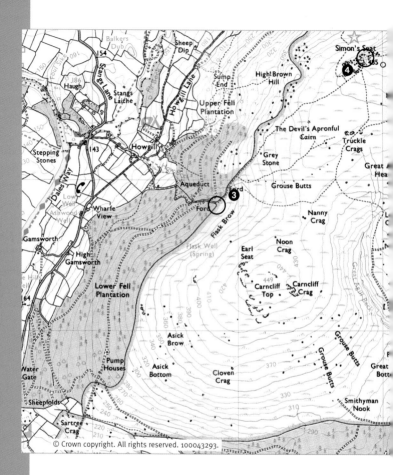

who found an abandoned baby here.

The moors of Barden Fell which spread out to the south of Simon's Seat are used for grouse shooting and belong to the Bolton Abbey estate. In times past members of the public had to apply for permits to walk on these moors. In 1968, however, a formal access

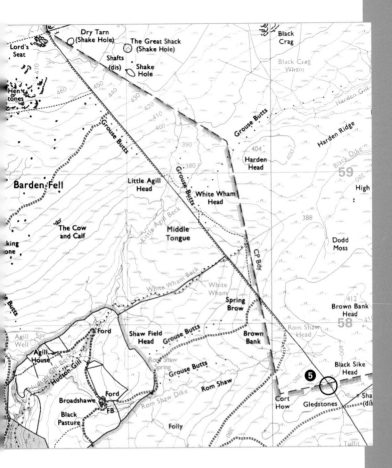

agreement was signed for parts of both Barden Fell and Barden Moor (to the west of the Wharfe), and this was followed by two further agreements in 1970 and 1974. Despite the powers made available to the national park under the National Parks and Access to the Countryside Act 1949, these were effectively the only access agreements to be negotiated in the Yorkshire Dales.

▶ From Simon's Seat follow the flagged track towards nearby Lord's Seat, another outcrop of rocks. Beyond the boundary wall here, if you fancy more moorland walking, it's possible to continue on open country towards the Great Pock Stones and Pock

Stones Moor. (Alternatively, the quickest way home from Simon's Seat is down the well-walked track which runs south, close to Great Agill Beck, to the so-called Valley of Desolation).

The suggested route, however, turns south-east at Lord's Seat, following the fell wall down the hillside to White Wham Beck, losing more than 375 ft (115 m) in height in the process. After a

On Barden Fell

short boggy stretch, most of the way is on a very pleasant grassy shooting track.

Continue beyond the turf-roofed shooters' hut at the bottom and climb up the hillside ahead, still keeping close to the wall. Unless you are anxious to get home, it's worth ignoring the first track off to the right to reach the brow ❺ and savour the views which (weather permitting) open up over Blubberhouses Moor. After a few yards of rough ground, turn right on to another shooting track and follow this back over the brow of the hill. Simon's Seat is once more in view ahead.

Leave the track just beyond the wall at Hammerthorn Gate to head again across open ground, making for the little-visited trig point just to the west ❻.

From here, some walkers may choose to head north-westwards to arrive above the picturesque waterfalls on Posforth Gill. To continue, however, involves a steep scramble down hill and a potentially tricky fording of the river just below the falls. The suggested route from the trig point, therefore, is south-west to the fine outcrop of rocks at South Nab ❼ and then in a roughly westerly direction to meet the footpath along Posforth Gill ½ mile (0.8 km) or so downstream from the waterfalls. Don't worry that the land south of South Nab is not shown as access land on OS maps; it remains, in fact, access land under the previous voluntary agreement.

■ Posforth Gill was renamed the Valley of Desolation after a bad storm in 1826 tore down trees and caused a flood. The name evokes the romantic approach which early nineteenth-century visitors to the countryside near Bolton Abbey brought to nature and the landscape.

▶ Follow the path down to the road near Posforth Bridge. Cross the footbridge over the Wharfe, back to the Cavendish Pavilion.

Nidderdale

When the Yorkshire Dales became a national park in 1954, Nidderdale was the dale which was left out in the cold. Despite its beauty, despite its historical links with the other dales to the west and north and its right to be considered as much a part of the Yorkshire Dales region as Wharfedale, Wensleydale or Swaledale, the boundary for the national park was drawn firmly along the Great Whernside watershed. Nidderdale, it seemed, was officially not worthy of national park status.

This was always nonsense, of course, a piece of gerrymandering most likely undertaken because neither Bradford Corporation's water board (which owned the moors used for water collection above Scar House reservoir) nor the large shooting estates which ringed Nidderdale particularly wanted the restrictions which might have come along with national park status. The official line was that Nidderdale was too industrialized – though this didn't stop the old lead-mining areas of Swaledale or Grassington Moor or the coalfields of Arkengarthdale from being welcomed into the national park.

Being outside the national park did indeed mean that there were fewer restrictions, such as planning controls, imposed in Nidderdale. But there was a downside, too. Nidderdale began to miss out on some of the economic and social benefits which came from being part of a national park. And in any case by the early 1990s it was becoming increasingly clear that the lack of official recognition for Nidderdale's landscapes and heritage was an anomaly which needed to be corrected.

Some argued that the answer would be to extend the national park's boundaries eastwards to absorb Nidderdale. But the eventual solution was more of a compromise. In 1994 it was agreed that Nidderdale would become England's thirty-sixth Area of Outstanding Natural Beauty (AONB). The AONB includes the upper Nidd valley, Fountains Abbey, much of Blubberhouses Moor, the fascinating outcrop of Brimham Rocks, the interesting old town of Pateley Bridge and smaller communities such as Kirkby Malzeard.

If national parks are the Premiership when it comes to the official designation of landscapes, AONBs are considered one league down in the beauty stakes. They have greater protection than regions with no designation at all (an important point when, for example, it comes to decisions on the siting of wind farms), but nevertheless they do not have the statutory powers which national park authorities are given in areas such as planning.

Despite the limitations, a small team of officers, mostly employed under the auspices of Harrogate Borough Council, staff the Nidderdale AONB office in Pateley Bridge. They co-ordinate a range of projects, for example to encourage local businesses to support sustainable tourism initiatives in the area. The AONB office has also built up a team of local conservation volunteers who help out regularly with such activities as footpath improvements, woodland management and scrub clearance.

With the passing of the Countryside and Rights of Way Act 2000, the open moorland of Nidderdale is now available for all to enjoy. The AONB team has erected a number of information boards for visitors at the edge of open country, and also fields a team of volunteer rangers at weekends. But there is perhaps still unfinished business, particularly as some potential concessionary routes across non-access land into open country remain to be negotiated. The fine moors to the west of Gouthwaite reservoir, for instance, remain difficult for walkers to reach from the main road through the dale. Access, it has to be said, is not a development which every landowner in the area has been particularly keen to welcome.

· WALK 9

THE GREAT WHERNSIDE RIDGE FROM NIDDERDALE

DIFFICULTY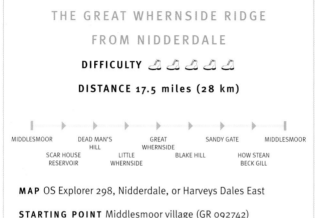

DISTANCE 17.5 miles (28 km)

MIDDLESMOOR — DEAD MAN'S HILL — GREAT WHERNSIDE — SANDY GATE — MIDDLESMOOR
SCAR HOUSE RESERVOIR — LITTLE WHERNSIDE — BLAKE HILL — HOW STEAN BECK GILL

MAP OS Explorer 298, Nidderdale, or Harveys Dales East

STARTING POINT Middlesmoor village (GR 092742)

PUBLIC TRANSPORT Summer buses run from Pateley Bridge (with connections to major West Yorkshire cities) on Sundays and Bank Holidays.

PARKING In the Middlesmoor car park, beyond the village. If walking the shorter route (see below), you may wish to park at Scar House reservoir.

A substantial hike around the head of Nidderdale to Little Whernside and Great Whernside, followed by the wild and lonely landscapes of Riggs Moor. Straightforward navigation, except in poor visibility when the walk is not recommended. For a shorter walk, though still one of significant length, make your way cross-country off the top of Great Whernside, aiming for the southern side of Angram reservoir.

■ Middlesmoor is an attractive village high up on a promontory between the Nidd and How Stean valleys. The church in particular occupies an impressive position. Although the church was rebuilt in Victorian times its dedication to the seventh-century bishop St Chad suggests that this has long been a Christian site. Some believe that the church was built on what had previously been a pagan place of worship.

Inside the church is an Anglo-Saxon cross, which probably dates back to the eleventh century.

▶ From Middlesmoor walk along the track which starts where the tarmac road stops, enjoying the views to the left over the valley of How Stean Beck. As Scar House reservoir comes into sight, drop down to cross the reservoir dam ❶.

■ Scar House reservoir, together with Angram reservoir which is situated even higher up the Nidd valley, was built by Bradford Corporation early in the twentieth century to meet the water needs of the city. The Nidd Aqueduct (see page 135) carries water from the reservoirs more than thirty miles (forty-eight kilometres) through an underground network to treatment works north-west of the city.

Angram reservoir was completed in 1919 and Scar House, about double the size of Angram with a total water capacity of over two billion gallons, was finished in 1936. Unlike most reservoir dams in Yorkshire, which are made of compacted earth with a central clay layer to prevent water seepage, the dams at Angram and Scar House are of concrete construction, faced with masonry. Scar House dam measures 233 ft (71 m) high.

During the construction of the reservoirs, a 'village' was built just below the

▶ Map continues westwards on pages 118–19

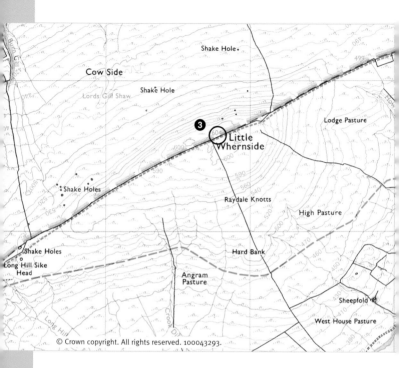

Scar House dam to provide accommodation for the workforce. The community was equipped with a cinema, a concert hall and a hospital.

▶ After crossing the dam, continue on the well-defined track which runs westwards a little above the reservoir to a ruined settlement at Lodge.

■ Although you wouldn't choose to bring a Mini this way, this track is one of those Dales 'green lanes' where motor cars and motor bikes are legally permitted to come (see page 32). The track is an old highway that once linked upper Nidderdale and upper Coverdale.

Sadly, not every traveller

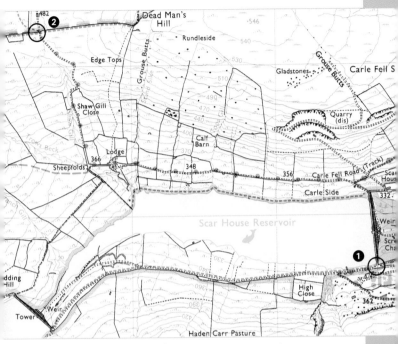

▶ Map continues westwards on page 120

in times past made the journey safely. In May 1728 three murdered bodies were discovered buried on the moor near Lodge End, the find being made more gruesome by the fact that the victims' heads had been cut off. The most likely explanation seems to be that they were Scottish pedlars who had been robbed for their money. The discovery is recalled in the name Dead Man's Hill.

▶ Past Lodge, turn right following the track up the flank of Dead Man's Hill. At the top ❷, turn left to follow the fence line to the summit of Little Whernside ❸.

■ Little Whernside is a fine-looking hill from a distance but rather more disappointing at close hand. For well over ½ mile (more than 1 km), the walking becomes hard work, as you encounter deep peat bogs. Persevere close to the fence as best you can. The good news is that this stretch is as bad as it gets.

The ridge from Little Whernside to Great Whernside was the historic county boundary between the West Riding and the North Riding, and it still marks the limit of the Yorkshire Dales National Park.

It is also, not surprisingly, a parish boundary. A carved boundary stone can be found half-hidden in the peat shortly after you drop down from Little Whernside; it is marked with an S on one side and a C on the other, the letters standing for the two parishes of Stonebeck Up and Carlton Highdale.

The ridge walk was formally dedicated as a right of way only in the late 1990s, thanks to the efforts of Rodney Waddilove and fellow members of the Harrogate branch of the Ramblers' Association and to the co-operation of Yorkshire Water (see page 79).

▶ Carry on past the head of the River Nidd to Black Dike End, and continue to the summit cairn on Great Whernside ❹.

Continue south for a few hundred yards (metres), until you meet the boundary fence at the second cairn shown on the OS map. Turn left and follow the fence past Stone Head Crag on to the wild expanses of Riggs Moor.

The walk stays alongside this fence for the next 3 miles (5 km) or so. Even in good weather, this moor feels remote and forgotten, a long way from the landscapes more commonly associated with the Yorkshire Dales. The only company hereabouts is likely to be the set of boundary stones marked WH 1863, encountered in the stretch around Blake Hill ❺.

▶ page 124

▶ Map continues eastwards on pages 122–3

⑧

▶ Eventually, at a stile at Sandy Gate ❻, you meet the path between Middlesmoor and Conistone in Wharfedale. Turn left on to the footpath, and follow it as it contours around the hillside above Straight Stean Beck. Beyond is the distinctive conical peak of Meugher, home to one of the loneliest trig points in the Dales.

Shortly after the first sheepfold ❼, the obvious route to follow is the water company track, although the right of way is shown on the map as being slightly higher up the hillside.

■ When Scar House and Angram reservoirs were being planned, Bradford Corporation chose not to build a companion reservoir in the How Stean valley. The corporation did, however, undertake significant engineering works to ensure that almost all the water which falls in the catchment area of How Stean Beck – and in total there's a lot of it – is captured, combined with water from the moors directly above the two reservoirs and sent on its way down the Nidd Aqueduct to Bradford.

How Stean Beck valley has been left, therefore, as a kind of 'virtual' reservoir with an impressive (if not always immediately attractive) infrastructure of bridges, weirs and buried pipework.

▶ Keep to the water company track, turning right at a junction to pass the ruins of High Riggs. Enter the farmyard of Low Riggs ❽, pass to the immediate right of the farm building through a gate and follow a field path through several other gates down to the river valley.

At this point cross the bridge and keep to the footpath as it climbs diagonally up the hillside. At a junction of paths, take the middle path (heading roughly straight ahead) and follow it across fields back to the village of Middlesmoor.

■ After the wild moorland of Riggs Moor, this final part of the walk is a pastoral delight. As a (slightly further) alternative, the right-hand path at the junction offers a route back to Middlesmoor via How Stean Gorge. This impressive limestone canyon carved out by the river is in places 80 ft (25 m) deep. The gorge can be admired from public rights of way, though access to the paths into the gorge itself is subject to a charge. A popular visitor attraction, How Steam Gorge also offers a café which weary walkers may well appreciate.

Gouthwaite reservoir, Nidderdale

WALK 10

VISITING JENNY TWIGG (AND TIB)

DIFFICULTY 👢 👢 👢 **DISTANCE 8 miles (13 km)**

| SCAR HOUSE ROAD | THROPE EDGE | JENNY TWIGG AND TIB | THROPE EDGE | SCAR HOUSE ROAD |
| MANCHESTER HOLE AND GOYDEN POT | OUSTER BANK | SYPELAND CRAGS | THROPE | |

MAP OS Explorer 298, Nidderdale, or Harveys Dales East

STARTING POINT 'Old tunnel' car park on the Yorkshire Water road leading to Scar House reservoir (GR 099765)

PUBLIC TRANSPORT Summer buses from Pateley Bridge (with connections to major West Yorkshire cities) run on Sundays and Bank Holidays. Alight at either Lofthouse or Middlesmoor and take field footpaths (adding 4 miles/6.4 km to the distance).

PARKING There is room for about six cars to park.

Jenny Twigg stands upright beside her daughter Tib on the moors above Nidderdale. This walk offers a chance to visit them, combined with spectacular hilltop views of the valley of the young Nidd.

■ The Yorkshire Water road to Scar House reservoir leaves the main upper Nidderdale road just past Lofthouse. As the blocked tunnel by the parking space suggests, this road was originally a light railway, built at the time when the two reservoirs at the head of the Nidd valley were being constructed.

Unusually for a contractor's railway, the line from Pateley Bridge as far as Lofthouse was also open to passengers, as the Nidd Valley Light Railway. Passenger traffic ran only until 1929, however.

▶ Take the path from the car park straight down to the Nidd river and cross the stones. The impressive cavern opposite is Manchester Hole.

■ Manchester Hole offers access to one of the most popular caving systems in the Dales, as the minibuses often parked on the road here testify. Much of the River Nidd dives underground a few yards (metres) upstream, and can be seen and heard rushing along at the bottom of the cave.

From here, cavers have a number of options. Traditionally, a through trip from Manchester Hole involved a relatively short journey: first to the so-called Main Chamber and then by means of tight crawls through river passages to emerge at

Bax Pot near Goyden Pot, a short distance downstream. Cavers have now found ways of linking together the Manchester Hole and Goyden Pot systems, and the new connections offer considerably longer excursions underground. Today the experienced caver can spend several hours squeezing through boulder chokes, crawling along passages and tackling rope pitches. However, the cave systems flood easily and can only be safely tackled when water levels are low or normal.

▶ Walk alongside the river downstream, continuing past Goyden Pot to reach Limley Farm ❶.

■ Unless water levels are particularly high, this will be a riverside walk without a river. The Nidd here does its most spectacular disappearing act, slipping away underground. One moment there is water beside the river bank; a moment later the water has been replaced by a stony river bed. Limley Farm itself is cosily enfolded by a dry river.

▶ Walk through Limley Farm, following waymarks, to find the path up the hill to Thwaite. Just beyond Thwaite, turn right. A bridleway (barely visible on the ground) runs eastwards towards a field barn at the edge of open country ❷.

■ Thwaite is a Norse name meaning either a clearing or – equally appropriate here – a field which slopes down to a valley. The name suggests that this farm has a history which goes back for well over a millennium.

▶ From the back of the barn, head diagonally right up the hillside following a trod. Continue along Thrope Edge past rocky outcrops, making for the shooting house ahead on the moor edge ❸. This building manages to look faintly ecclesiastical, an unlikely church dedicated to the pursuit of grouse shooting.

■ The views which gradually emerge as you climb the hillside must be some of the finest in the Dales. Little

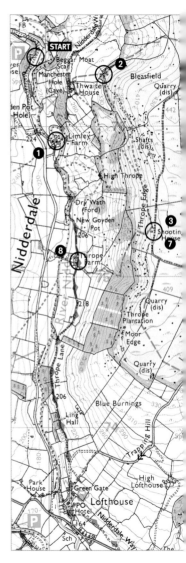

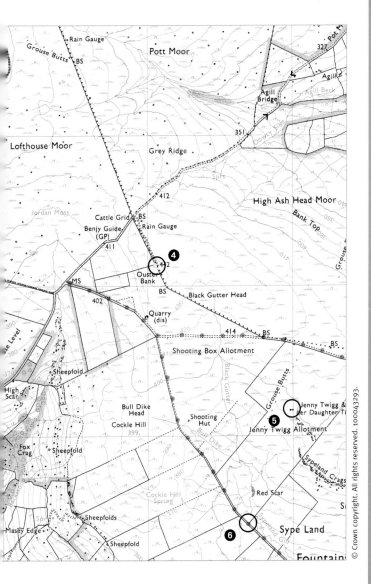

Whernside, at the head of the dale, closes off the view nicely to the west, with the whole horseshoe ridge of Little Whernside, Great Whernside and Meugher visible by the time you reach the brow of the hill. Further away to the south-west is the prominent high ground of Thrope Fell Top on Barden Moor (Walk 7). Nidderdale, lying below, is itself a particularly attractive valley.

▶ Turn away from the hillside edge to follow the track eastwards. Cross the minor road and briefly take the rough road opposite before cutting across to the trig point at Ouster Bank ❹.

■ At this point there are also views eastwards, down towards the less hilly countryside of lower Wensleydale.

▶ From the trig point follow the wall south and east over Black Gutter Head, to rejoin briefly the moorland road towards Ilton. Just past a small shooting hut turn right on to open country,

Jenny Twigg and her daughter

following a track down past grouse butts. Ahead, unmistakable on the moorland, are the impressive twin pillars, Jenny Twigg and her daughter Tib **⑤**.

■ With Jenny Twigg and Tib, some of the magic of Easter Island arrives in the land of millstone grit. (No wonder Henry Moore's work was influenced by the landscapes of his native Yorkshire.)

At some stage in history, presumably, someone decided that these two pillars were mother and daughter, and that their names were to be Jenny Twigg and Tib. It has been suggested that 'Jenny' may conceivably refer to the fairy Gennett or Janet whose waterfall near Malham is a well-known visitor attraction (Walk 1).

Until the introduction of access legislation in 2005, Jenny and Tib were on private moorland and not officially open to visits from the public.

▶ Follow the trod from Jenny Twigg and Tib south-east to explore the impressive rocky outcrop of Sypeland Crags. Then cut down across Sype Land to pick up another moor road just beyond Sypeland Gill **⑥**. Head back to the shooting house **⑦** and this time turn straight down the hillside, taking the bridleway which leads to Thrope Farm **⑧**. At the farm turn north, following the waymarked Nidderdale Way.

■ Another sign that much of the action in this part of Nidderdale is happening underground is an entrance to the Goyden Pot/New Goyden Pot caving system, which is passed just north of Thrope Farm. Somewhat incongruously, the system is entered through a drop, capped with a metal lid, which is sited right in the middle of the river bed – just where the Nidd would be if it hadn't chosen, like cavers, to disappear at this point below the surface.

▶ Return past Limley Farm to the start of the walk.

From reservoir to tap

The map isn't available to tourists or printed on the back of guidebooks, but the Yorkshire Dales has its own underground network which is almost as complicated (and, those in the know would say, just as important) as London's Underground.

Beneath the heather and grass, far below the rabbit runs, is a man-made system of tunnels. The occasional clues on the surface to this subterranean world are not necessarily easy to spot. Take, for example, the curious little stone-faced building with a well-padlocked metal door on an isolated hilltop east of Stump Cross Caverns. Most people, if they noticed it, would probably assume that this building is a relic of the lead-mining industry that flourished on these hillsides for centuries. Just occasionally, however, the padlock will be opened, the door swung open and the contents of the building revealed to be a large circular concrete air shaft. Whatever the weather, a cold blast of air will be rising up the shaft from far out of sight below.

This shaft is one of a number which reach down to the Greenhow tunnel, which at its deepest is some 400 ft (120 m) below the ground. The tunnel is perhaps the most impressive part of a feat of engineering linking the head of Nidderdale with northern Bradford, about thirty miles or so away.

This vital artery is known as the Nidd Aqueduct, and without it the taps in Bradford would very quickly run dry. Bradford Corporation built Angram and Scar House, the two large reservoirs at the head of the upper Nidd valley, early in the twentieth century and between them they store over three billion gallons of water, ready to be turned into drinking water. But the building of the reservoirs was only half the story. Bradford Corporation then had to arrange for the water to be conveyed to where it was needed: the Nidd Aqueduct, in other words, also had to be constructed.

The aqueduct starts just to the south-east of the Scar House dam in a small Yorkshire Water building closed to the public (it is next to the building marked on maps as 'screening chamber'). From here water is carried ultimately to the treatment works at Chellow Heights, to the north-west of Bradford city centre, a journey which typically takes about eighteen hours. Impressively, the aqueduct was constructed to operate entirely by gravity, without recourse to pumping stations. This meant the need in places for deep tunnels like that at Greenhow, which carries water out of the Nidd valley system into the Wharfe valley.

It also meant devising a method of getting water down and then up the sides of valleys encountered along the way. Here the answer was to use the siphon technique, albeit on a somewhat larger scale than dreamed of by most people when they try to make a siphon with a piece of garden hose. In upper Nidderdale alone, siphons are used to carry the Nidd Aqueduct across How Stean Beck, Ramsgill Beck, Burn Gill and Ashfordside Beck.

The quantity of water which flows from Angram and Scar House is decided by Chellow Heights' estimation of the amount it needs to treat for Yorkshire Water's customers. However, there are restrictions. Yorkshire Water has a water extraction licence issued by the Environment Agency, which sets an upper limit for the amount of water that can be taken from the Nidd Aqueduct. The unit of measurement used is the tcmd (thousand cubic metres per day) and – of course you want to know – the current limit stands at 113,000 tcmd. To check that it is obeying the terms of its licence, Yorkshire Water has what amounts to a very big water meter on the aqueduct, sited in a building in Burn Gill west of Gouthwaite reservoir. Fortunately, its engineers can monitor the readings remotely (and if need be close and open valves to regulate the flow), using a sophisticated computer telemetry network.

The Nidd Aqueduct is the largest and most impressive tunnel system in the southern Dales (it's possible to stand upright inside the Greenhow tunnel, for example – not that this would be advisable when the water is flowing), but it is just one of a series of similar underground networks which carry the waters off the Dales towards the cities. Upper and Lower Barden reservoirs (Walk 7) have their own Barden culvert which ultimately deposits their water at Graincliffe reservoir, on the south side of Ilkley Moor north of Bingley. Rivers are also used as part of the network. For example, water from Grimwith reservoir is released into the River Dibb, which in turn enters the River Wharfe. A similar amount of water is then extracted from the Wharfe downstream at Lobwood near Addingham, and sent on to nearby Chelker reservoir before in turn being passed down to Chellow Heights.

Yorkshire Water has teams of engineers in what it calls its Head Works Division to ensure that everything is done to keep the water flowing. Although telemetry (literally, taking measurements from a distance) means that much of the work can be controlled remotely via computer, it is still necessary to check on the ground that the systems are functioning correctly, and Yorkshire Water's Land Rovers regularly have to bump their way up and down remote tracks to take staff on-site. Dams are subject to safety checks every few days and, periodically, the tunnels, culverts and catchwater channels have to be inspected and, when necessary, repaired or cleaned out.

Fortunately, the nineteenth- and twentieth-century workers and engineers who built the reservoirs and aqueducts built them to last. It's an achievement which sometimes we can take just a little too much for granted.

WALK 11

DALLOWGILL

DIFFICULTY 👟 👟 **DISTANCE** 6½ miles (10.5 km)

HARPER HILL · DALLOW · DALLOWGILL · KETTLESTANG · HARPER HILL

MAP OS Explorer 298, Nidderdale, or Harveys Dales East

STARTING POINT On the minor road between Kirkby Malzeard and Patcley Bridge, near the junction with the lane from High Grantley (GR 195703)

PUBLIC TRANSPORT While there are no easy public transport options, at the time of publication a community bus service (Ripon Roweller) connects Ripon to the village of High Grantley (about 2½ miles/4 km from the start of the walk) twice a day, Monday–Saturday. Dalesbus 802 (summer Sundays/Bank Holidays) from Wakefield/Leeds passes about 3 miles (5 km) to the south of the walk start, as does the occasional 812 service from York (also summer Sundays/Bank Holidays).

PARKING A small number of cars can park informally on the road verge near the entrance to Harper Hill Farm.

This pleasant walk in a little-known but beautiful corner of Yorkshire combines upland pastureland with some moorland walking on newly accessible Dallowgill Moor. Relatively easy walking on footpaths and shooting tracks, with 1 mile (1.6 km) or so of somewhat rougher terrain.

Dallowgill Moor is an important bird-nesting area, used not only by grouse but by other ground-nesting birds. You may want to consider avoiding this route during the nesting season.

■ Before starting out, take a moment to look across Dallowgill Moor to the distinctive white building in the distance to the west. This is Kettlestang shooting house, one of the objectives of the walk. If the cloud is down and Kettlestang is not visible, be aware that the walk may require some compass navigation.

▶ Walk along the road for a few yards (metres), crossing the cattle grid. Turn left, following the signposted track across the moor towards Dallow.

■ This area of moor is known as Coal Hill and the coarse coal is easy to spot, breaking out of the ground beneath your feet. The coal was mined on nearby Skelding Moor.

▶ When you reach the lane near Dallow, turn left and follow it past Dallow Hall ❶ and the attractive cottages beyond. Continue on the track, keeping to the right of way which runs beside the edge of the woods.

■ Just as the woods begin, look out for the mosaic set in a large stone among the trees on your right. This is the first of a number of mosaic panels which add interest and enjoyment to the initial part of the walk.

It was in 1996 that a group of people who lived in and around Kirkby Malzeard came together to plan a mosaic trail around Dallowgill. The aim of their project was to celebrate the designation of Nidderdale as an Area of Outstanding Natural Beauty (see page 113).

Under the supervision of artist Margaret Murphy, the Crackpots, as the group named itself, produced a total of twenty-two ceramic panels which are now in place beside footpaths in the area.

This first ceramic mosaic, *Fungi*, is by Gwynneth Jackson. You will find a second mosaic, *Deer* by Wahneta Thorne, after a further 200 yards (200 m) or so, just beyond the first stream.

▶ Follow the path down beside the wood, turning right over the stream to climb up the other side.

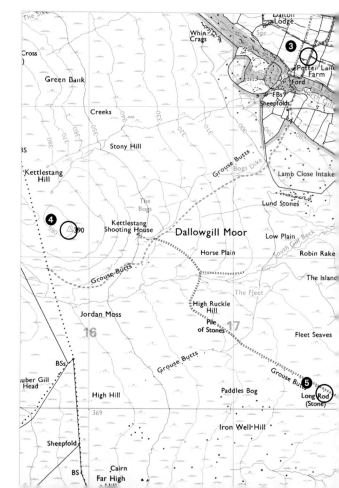

Near the top, before Glebe Farm, turn left across a stile **2**.

■ This next section includes both woodland and pasture, with attractive views down across Dallowgill towards the moors beyond. Kettlestang shooting house, with a clump of trees beside it, comes into sight again.

There are three more ceramic mosaics to watch out for here. The first, *Rabbits* by

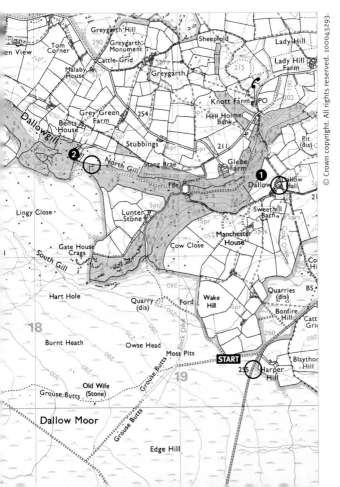

James Stewart, is beside the first stile. Shortly afterwards, at the entrance to the woods, is *Barn Owl* by Patrice Lyth. Finally, *Bents House* by Frances Lyth is to be found at the entrance to the farmhouse which carries its name.

To visit all twenty-two ceramics would involve completing the Crackpots Trail, a route of 7½ miles (12 km) mainly to the north and east of Dallowgill. The Nidderdale AONB office has produced an illustrated guide to the trail.

▶ Continue on the footpath past Bents House and the barn beyond. Turn left when you reach the track to Potter Lane Farm ❸.

Continue down the sunken lane to the east and south of Potter Lane Farm (this section can be boggy), to cross the small bridge over North Gill Beck. Follow the farm track briefly, before (as the track turns right) crossing a wall ahead into a small pasture.

The right of way runs through a further small field before crossing by a gate, to the left of a ruined building, into the larger area of Lamb Close Intake. Follow the now well-defined track, in due course turning right through another gate and on to the open moor.

■ This right of way was, until 2005, a cul-de-sac leading up to, but no further than, the parish boundary high on the moors near Kettlestang Hill. As such, and not surprisingly, it was hardly walked. However, the firmness and definition of the track under foot, particularly the stretch through Lamb Close Intake, reveals that this was indeed an historic route crossing the moor.

In his book *Roads and Trackways of the Yorkshire Dales* (1985), Geoffrey Wright describes this route as an old road which ran across Dallowgill and Sigsworth Moors from Potter Lane to the village of Wath in Nidderdale. As he points out, the section on Sigsworth Moor has now been lost.

He quotes, however, the nineteenth-century historian William Grainge who recorded in 1863 that the old road there was four feet wide and paved with stones. 'It may, therefore, have been a medieval causeway of monastic days,' Geoffrey Wright concludes.

Almost certainly, the full length of the road should have been registered as a right of way – and arguably as a bridleway, rather than a footpath – when the definitive rights-of-way map for the area was first being produced. The concept of a definitive map was introduced by Parliament in the National Parks and Access to the Countryside Act 1949 (before then, court action was the only way to establish that a path was available for public use).

However, not all historic routes found their way on to the maps. In some areas (as here) a traditional right of way became arbitrarily amputated at a parish boundary, being registered only on one side of the divide.

The Countryside and Rights of Way Act 2000 introduced a cut-off date of 2026, after which it will no longer be possible to add historic routes (those which existed before 1949) to definitive maps. The Ramblers' Association has pointed out to its members that there is therefore some urgency in ensuring that long-established rights are not extinguished for ever after 2026. 'If you have a claim based on documentary evidence, then the message is very much to get your claim in,' urges the Ramblers' Association.

▶ The path now crosses the open moor, running beside Bogs Dike towards Kettlestang shooting house. From here, it is worth venturing the short distance to enjoy the view from the trig point on the top of Kettlestang Hill ❹.

■ The golf-ball-shaped radomes of Menwith Hill, the United States' controversial telecommunications interception centre near Blubberhouses (and a place of frequent peace demonstrations), can be seen to the south. A little further eastwards, appearing from a distance almost like a fortified castle, is a natural landmark: the impressive rocky outcrops of Brimham Rocks, now owned by the National Trust.

▶ Take the shooting track back from the shooting house and follow it as it runs south-eastwards across the heather moor, past the standing stone known as Long Rod ❺.

■ These moors form part of the Dallowgill estate and are managed for grouse shooting. As well as encouraging the red grouse, which will keep walkers company for the next few miles, the Dallowgill estate has tried in recent years to entice the much rarer black grouse to return to this area. Among other initiatives, the estate has attempted to recreate areas of scrub and native woodland, which is the habitat favoured by the black grouse.

▶ From Long Rod, the easiest route back is to continue on the shooting tracks, turning left after a short while. Alternatively, to

save a little distance, cut across open country making for a line of grouse butts. Follow the path beside the butts down to join the shooting track near a second prominent stone, Old Wife (also known locally as Batty Wife). Return to the road at Harper Hill.

Brimham Rocks

Battling for the buses

It began, like many things do in Britain, with a discussion in the pub. The year was 1996 and a small group of regular bus users had got together to talk tactics. The public transport network in the Dales was, little by little, being cut back and bus routes into Nidderdale and upper Swaledale were at immediate risk of being lost. A few more years, the group reasoned over their pints, and the beauties of much of the Dales could be lost for good to anyone who didn't have access to a car.

What was needed, they decided, was a new group, a campaigning body which could stir things up, attract the attention of the media and embarrass the authorities into taking public transport more seriously. And so it came about: the Yorkshire Dales Public Transport Users Group, or YDPTUG, was born. The first twenty or so members quickly signed themselves up. Encouraged and supported by the admirable Yorkshire Dales Society (who also campaign for sustainable travel to the Yorkshire Dales), the group soon began to flourish.

YDPTUG may not be the most elegant acronym, but this hasn't stopped the group from rapidly making its mark, with membership now around 450. Over the years there have been more battles to defend threatened bus services and several occasions when the group has had to use all its campaigning experience to influence the decision makers. More often than not, this seems to work. As one founder member puts it, 'The group's regarded with fear and trepidation by the Park authorities.'

But it has not all been negative. Increasingly, YDPTUG has been able to work for improvements to the bus network. In 2004 it went a step further, actually taking on the role of bus contractor and signing up a local coach operator to ensure the continuation over the winter months of the popular Sunday

805 service from York and Leeds through Wharfedale to Hawes. Perhaps not surprisingly, passenger numbers rapidly increased after YDPTUG took charge of the route.

The 805, and other similar routes such as the 800 and 803, are seen as particularly important in ensuring that the beautiful countryside of the Yorkshire Dales is available to all. These routes provide direct links between the large industrial cities and the heart of the Dales. They mean that you can jump on a bus in places like Leeds, or Bradford, or Wakefield, or Darlington, and stay put while the scenery outside changes from urban sprawl to rural splendour. They also mean that you can get back home at the end of the day. Wharfedale, Wensleydale and Swaledale are all served, at least in the summer, by these long-distance bus routes.

As well as the more popular dales, hidden Nidderdale has been a particular focus for YDPTUG's attentions over the years. The buses up the narrow road from Pateley Bridge to Middlesmoor and Lofthouse provide a lifeline for local residents and also have the important additional advantage of giving walkers access to the lovely countryside at the head of the valley. But, apart from the high road to Masham, upper Nidderdale is a dead end and it's also outside the Dales national park boundary – both factors which could count against provision of a decent bus service.

As mentioned above, it was the threat of cutbacks to Nidderdale buses which helped bring about YDPTUG's creation. Nothing daunted, YDPTUG rapidly got to work. In 1997 it produced its first Nidderdale Public Transport Survey, a twenty-six page document designed to make the local authorities take note. A year later, reinforced with analysis of data from a questionnaire, a second report was produced. The year after that, the group published yet another report. All this spadework has paid off: in 2003, YDPTUG was able to publish for the first time the full-colour *Explore Nidderdale* booklet, available free to visitors and giving details both of bus times and places to visit. *Explore Nidderdale* is now a regular fixture in tourist information centres across the region.

YDPTUG has some very keen walkers among its members, so it's hardly surprising that one of the group's more recent initiatives has been to launch its own programme of guided walks. Dalesbus Ramblers organize walks throughout the year and welcome all. Details are posted on a dedicated website www.dalesbusramblers.co.uk – and it goes without saying that every walk begins and ends at a bus stop.

Transport is an important issue for every national park, and the growth in the number of cars on the roads is increasingly forcing the subject up the political agenda. The talk now in the Yorkshire Dales is of trying to establish long-term sustainable alternatives to the private car. YDPTUG is a key member of the newly formed Yorkshire Dales Sustainable Travel Partnership, where it sits across the table from local authorities, the national park authority, the government regional office and the bus and train operators. One of the aims is to develop a more strategic approach to public transport in the Dales, so that bus services are not each year at risk from funding cutbacks. There's also the long-term vision of proper bus and train links, and of simpler and more affordable ticketing.

The story of how YDPTUG has grown into a successful campaigning body is a heartening one, demonstrating the way in which a little bit of citizen power can pay off when it comes to defending public services. But YDPTUG does not feel its work is over yet. The message to the author of this book was a simple one: put in our contact details (www.dalesbus.org) and encourage more people to sign up as members. And tell them, too, to use the buses.

WALK 12

ILTON MOOR AND THE DRUID'S TEMPLE

DIFFICULTY 🥾 🥾 🥾 **(can be reduced to** 🥾 🥾 **)**

DISTANCE 9 miles (14.5 km)

LEIGHTON RESERVOIR — SIGHTING TOWER — ILTON MOOR — SANDY HILL — ILTON — DRUID'S TEMPLE — LEIGHTON — LEIGHTON RESERVOIR

MAP OS Explorer 298, Nidderdale, or Harveys Dales East

STARTING POINT Leighton reservoir, on the road between Masham and Lofthouse (GR 156787)

PUBLIC TRANSPORT The nearest place served by buses is Masham, about 4 miles (6.4 km) away. Currently, the 803 Swaledale Explorer bus offers a once-a-month summer Sunday service from Leeds and Wakefield to Masham.

PARKING Although the car park marked on OS maps is private, for the use of anglers only, there is limited space for off-road parking near by. Off-road parking is also possible beside the reservoir a short distance further south (in the Lofthouse direction).

Who could resist the chance to visit Yorkshire's version of Stonehenge, a strange nineteenth-century folly of epic proportions?

This relatively straightforward walk combines lower-level (though still isolated) moorland with some pleasant country walking.

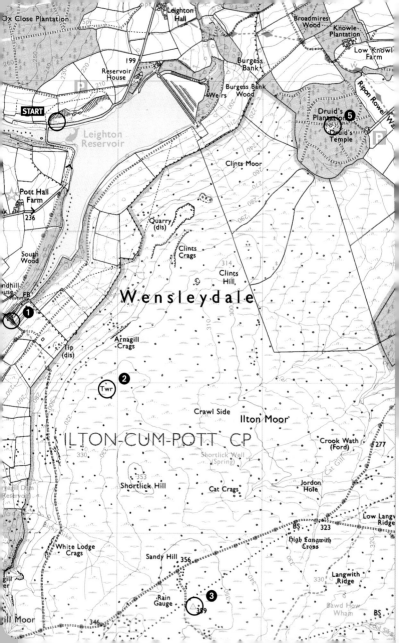

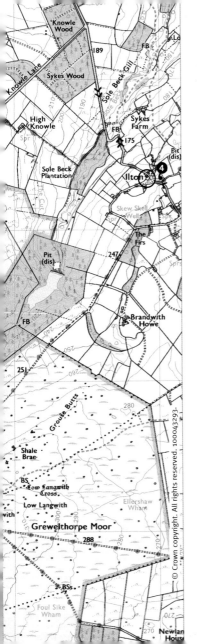

▶ Walk south from Leighton reservoir, taking the access lane which leads to the dam of next-door Roundhill reservoir.

■ Roundhill reservoir was built during the first years of the twentieth century, to supply water for Harrogate. The work took eleven years to complete and, as with other reservoir engineering projects, a narrow-gauge industrial railway was built to bring in materials, in this case from Masham about 7 miles (11 km) away.

Leighton reservoir followed a few years later, this time to meet the needs of the population of Leeds. The reservoir is stocked with brown and rainbow trout and is a popular place for fly fishermen.

▶ Cross the dam ❶, noting the fine tablets commemorating the construction of the reservoir. Beyond, follow the footpath up the hillside.

At the start of the moor, the suggested route (which involves 1 mile/1.6 km or so of rough walking) is to follow one of the faint trods south-eastwards, towards the tower at the top of the hill ❷. An alternative route, for a gentler, 'two-boot' walk, would be to take the footpath shown on the map (in reality, a pleasant green track) and follow it south past White Lodge Crags to meet the Ilton Moor shooting road.

■ The tower on Ilton Moor seems a curious construction, a strange sculptured folly with a hole for its heart. Its explanation is rather prosaic, however: it is a sighting tower, a memento of engineering works undertaken when the reservoirs were constructed in the valley below.

Sighting towers were a nineteenth-century device used, for example, in the construction of railway tunnels to ensure the correct line was taken. In this case the tower is a reminder of the Carlesmoor tunnel, yet another part of Yorkshire Water's subterranean network under the Dales (see page 135). The tunnel takes water from Roundhill south-eastwards to the hamlet of Carlesmoor near Kirkby Malzeard. Another sighting

tower can be found there (GR 195737).

▶ From the sighting tower, carry on southwards across the heather moor on to the high ground of Shortlick Hill, to meet the Ilton Moor road. (In bird-nesting season, it may be considered more responsible to return to find the footpath alternative.)

Continue to the trig point at Sandy Hill ❸, which offers extensive views over Kirkby Malzeard Moor to the south.

Return from the trig point to pick up the moor road, running eastwards through the heather. At the site of High Langwith Cross, take the left turn and head north-eastwards to Ilton.

■ High Langwith Cross was erected on the boundary of the Ilton-cum-Pott and Laverton parishes, and would have been a welcome landmark for moorland travellers in times past. Like other moorland crosses, the landmark has now disappeared. Nobody, it seems, has yet bothered to re-erect it.

▶ The moor road leads to the outskirts of the tiny community of Ilton. Turn left to find the lane to the village centre, such as it is ❹. Follow the by-road downhill to Sole Beck Gill and then turn left on to the footpath beside Sole Beck Plantation.

■ This path is part of Ripon Rowel Walk, a circular walk of 50 miles (80 km) devised by members of the Ramblers' Association in Ripon. A booklet on the route has been written by RA member Les Taylor.

▶ Beyond High Knowle stables, turn left on to Knowle Lane, to find the woods which contain the Druid's Temple ❺.

■ This magnificent folly is a one-off, an exuberant gothic celebration of a fake prehistory. Everything that can possibly be thought of gets a place here: there is a proper stone henge, far more complete than anything Wiltshire can provide, there are standing stones and megaliths, dolmens, a great slab of stone to serve as an altar and even a dark underground cave. Further stone dolmens are dotted about among the trees around the main 'temple'.

Although the Druid's Temple is one of the great follies of northern England, it is surprisingly little known outside the immediate Masham area. It was the creation of William Danby, the local landowner whose country house was nearby Swinton Park.

Danby, who was born in 1752 and died in 1833, seems to have been inspired in his project primarily by a desire to provide jobs for workers in the area at a time when unemployment was high. The Druid's Temple, therefore, could be deemed to be one of Britain's first job-creation projects. Certainly, no expense seems to have been spared in its construction.

William Danby inherited an estate which had been in the Danby family since the seventeenth century. As well as being responsible for the

Druid's Temple, he also added druidic follies and standing stones to the landscaped grounds surrounding the house (now an upmarket hotel). Another grandiose undertaking was the construction in the parkland of Quarry Gill Bridge, a gothic bridge which reputedly cost £11,000 – a staggering amount at the time.

▶ After exploring the woods of the Druid's Temple, return to pick up the Ripon Rowel Walk footpath across the fields to Leighton. This final stretch of the route makes a delightful country walk, with fine views towards the distant moors of lower Coverdale and Wensleydale in the north. Keep on the footpath as it drops down to the Pott Beck valley and then continues up to Leighton beyond. Return to the starting point.

The Druid's Temple

Some further reading

Bruce Bedford, *Underground Britain*, Willow Books, 1985

C.M.L. Bouch, *The Lady Anne*, self-published, 1954

D.J.H. Clifford (ed.), *The Diaries of Lady Anne Clifford*, Sutton Publishing, 1990

M.C. Gill, *The Wharfedale Mines*, British Mining No. 49, Northern Mine Research Society, 1994

Peter Gunn, *The Yorkshire Dales*, Century, 1984

Paul Hannon, *25 Walks: The Yorkshire Dales*, HMSO, 1996

Marie Hartley and Joan Ingilby, *Dales Memories*, Dalesman, 1986

Marie Hartley and Joan Ingilby, *The Yorkshire Dales*, Dent, 1956

Martin Holmes, *Proud Northern Lady*, Phillimore, 1975

Jack Keighley, *Walks in Dales Country*, Cicerone, 2000

David Leather, *Yorkshire Dales*, Collins, 2003

W.R. Mitchell, *High Dale Country*, Souvenir Press, 1991

W.R. Mitchell, *The Living Moors of Yorkshire*, Castleberg, 2002

Richard Muir, *The Dales of Yorkshire*, Macmillan, 1991

Arthur Raistrick, *Mines and Miners on Malham Moor*, George Kelsall, 1983

Arthur Raistrick, *West Riding of Yorkshire*, Hodder and Stoughton, 1970

Arthur Raistrick and Bernard Jennings, *A History of Lead Mining in the Pennines*, Longman, 1965

Colin Speakman, *Dales Way*, Dalesman, 1970

A. Wainwright, *In The Limestone Dales*, Michael Joseph, 1991

A. Wainwright, *On the Pennine Way*, Michael Joseph, 1985

A. Wainwright, *Pennine Way Companion*, new edition Frances Lincoln, 2003

A.C. Waltham, *Limestones and Caves of North-West England*, David and Charles, 1974

Tony Waltham, *Karst and Caves*, Yorkshire Dales National Park, 1987

Geoffrey Wright, *Roads and Trackways of the Yorkshire Dales*, Moorland, 1985

Geoffrey Wright, *The Yorkshire Dales*, David and Charles, 1986

The Countryside Code

An abbreviated version of the Countryside Code, launched in 2004 and supported by a wide range of countryside organizations including the Ramblers' Association, is given below.

Be safe – plan ahead and follow signs

Even when going out locally, it's best to get the latest information about where and when you can go; for example, your rights to enter some areas of open land may be restricted while work is being carried out, for safety reasons or during breeding seasons. Follow advice and local signs, and be prepared for the unexpected.

Leave gates and property as you find them

Please respect the working life of the countryside, as our actions can affect rural livelihoods, the safety and welfare of animals and people, and the heritage that belongs to all of us.

Protect plants and animals, and take your litter home

We have a responsibility to protect the countryside now and for future generations, so make sure you don't harm animals, birds, plants or trees.

Keep dogs under control

The countryside is a great place to exercise dogs, but it's every owner's duty to make sure their dog is not a danger or nuisance to farm animals, wildlife or other people.

Consider other people

Showing consideration and respect for other people makes the countryside a pleasant environment for everyone, whether they are at home, at work or at leisure.

Index